The Complete Guide to
Attics &
Basements

by Philip Schmidt
and Matthew Paymar

Creative Publishing
international

CHANHASSEN, MINNESOTA
www.creativepub.com

Creative Publishing
international

Copyright © 2007
Creative Publishing international, Inc.
18705 Lake Drive East
Chanhassen, Minnesota 55317
1-800-328-3895
www.creativepub.com

Printed in China

10 9 8 7 6 5 4 3 2 1

Library of Congress
Cataloging-in-Publication Data

Schmidt, Philip.
  The complete guide to attics & basements / by Philip
Schmidt and Matthew Paymar.
       p. cm.
  Summary: "For homeowners who need more living space
but aren't able or willing to move to a larger home or build an
expensive room addition. Shows how to add a bedroom,
bathroom, recreation room, or home office without changing
the basic blueprint of the home"--Provided by publisher.
  "Black and Decker."
  Includes index.
  ISBN-13: 978-1-58923-302-7 (soft cover)
  ISBN-10: 1-58923-302-6 (soft cover)
  1. Attics--Remodeling. 2. Basements--Remodeling. I.
Paymar, Matthew.
II. Title.

  TH4816.3.A77.S36 2007
  643'.5--dc22

2006100067

President/CEO: Ken Fund
VP for Sales & Marketing: Peter Ackroyd

Home Improvement Group

Publisher: Bryan Trandem
Managing Editor: Tracy Stanley
Senior Editor: Mark Johanson
Editor: Jennifer Gehlhar

Creative Director: Michele Lanci-Altomare
Senior Design Manager: Brad Springer
Design Managers: Jon Simpson, Mary Rohl

Director of Photography: Tim Himsel
Lead Photographer: Steve Galvin
Photo Coordinators: Julie Caruso, Joanne Wawra
Shop Manager: Randy Austin

Production Managers: Laura Hokkanen, Linda Halls

Authors: Philip Schmidt, Matthew Paymar
Editor: Andrew Karre

THE COMPLETE GUIDE TO ATTICS & BASEMENTS
Created by: The Editors of Creative Publishing international, Inc., in cooperation with Black & Decker.
Black & Decker® is a trademark of The Black & Decker Corporation and is used under license.

This book includes material previously published as IdeaWise: Basements & Attics (Creative Publishing international, 2003), and
Finishing Basements & Attics (Creative Publishing international, 2000).

Contents

Introduction

Is your house lacking just a little more space but you love it too much to think about moving? Has your life changed since you bought the house and now you find you need a home office for your freelance work or telecommuting, a place for the children in your life to play, or an extra bedroom for a relative? Or maybe now that your obligations have changed, you find yourself fantasizing about a space dedicated to your hobbies?

This book can help you determine how best to use your tantalizingly empty attic or basement, inspire you with great design ideas, and give you the practical how-to to tackle the projects on your own.

Over half of houses in North America are more than 30 years old. The attics and basements in these older homes are often significantly underutilized spaces. They stand hollow and empty or become cluttered storerooms where years' worth of broken furniture and boxes of old clothes gather dust. Even in new construction, attics and basements often are left unfinished so that the new homeowners can determine for themselves how best to incorporate the space.

Finishing your attic or basement is the easiest way to add living space to your home. With the basic structure already in place, there's little heavy construction or outdoor work required, and the project probably won't disrupt your daily life the way an addition would. Best of all, the potential square footage to be gained is significant.

Remodeling a basement or attic can also be accomplished for a fraction of the effort and cost of building an addition. Additions not only require a new foundation, but they involve erecting an entirely new structure. Basements and attics, on the other hand, are already enclosed, framed, and roofed, and the services are already wired and plumbed into the walls. In fact, it typically costs 50% less to refinish your basement and attic than to construct an addition, but the additional livable space greatly increases the value of your home.

Any type of room can be moved to an attic or basement. There are advantages and disadvantages to each location, depending on your needs for the space. We'll address those concerns in later chapters. But if you know you want to convert an unfinished basement or attic, there are a few important considerations: zoning and building limitations, initial planning, and design preferences.

Many neighborhoods are regulated by strict zoning ordinances that either prohibit expansion of a home's existing footprint or make the process of adding to your home a nightmare—another good reason to look to your basement or attic for remodeling rather than adding to your house.

While there are zoning regulations that apply to basements and attics as well, they are primarily related to safety and to the suitability of the space for conversion. For example, because there is a

difference between "active" and "inactive" weight, the regulations governing the size, spacing, and span of floor joists are stricter for habitable space than for storage space. Other regulations pertain more to comfort: with few exceptions, habitable rooms must have a minimum 70 sq. ft. of floor space and at least a 7 ft. ceiling. Make sure to work with your local building department to ensure that your basement or attic meets local building code requirements.

This book can guide you through the entire finishing project. It's divided into sections that represent the major stages of finishing unused spaces, including the most important step of all: planning. In successful basement and attic conversions, it takes careful planning to fit together the many elements while maximizing living space.

But in order to create a complete plan, you'll need to determine everything that's going into the project, and not all projects follow the same construction sequence. Therefore, it's a good idea to read through this book entirely before you begin construction.

Part of your planning will be determining how much of the work you'll do yourself and how much you'll hire professionals to do. For the most part, finishing an attic or basement can be an any-season project, giving you much greater flexibility than you would have when building an addition. Although attic and basement conversions are good do-it-yourself projects, few homeowners have the tools and skills required to complete all the tasks involved. Many hire professionals to help with the planning and design, as well as the physical work.

Regardless of who does what work, you'll need to get building permits for your project—for several reasons. First, it's the law. Getting caught without permits will result in fines from the city and possibly trouble with your insurance company. And work done without a permit can cause complications when you sell your house. Secondly, because it's the law, not having permits may make it difficult to find good contractors to work on your project (they can lose their licenses). Third, and most important, having permits means all your work will be inspected by building inspectors to make sure it meets local building code requirements. Unless you've worked as an electrician, plumber, carpenter, or engineer, you probably won't know some of the details that apply to your project—and neither this nor any other book can tell you everything. Building inspections will ensure your work is safe for you and your family.

Finally, for many people the most fun part of any remodel is planning the initial design. At this stage, play with any idea that suits your fancy. You may find that a detail that seemed too indulgent at first becomes so important to you that you are able to find a way to make it work.

Because basements and attics are separate from the rest of the house, the design does not necessarily have to respond to the thematic elements found on the main floors. You're free to be more adventurous or even whimsical with these spaces. Remember, it's your unique needs, interests, and lifestyle that will transform an unused basement or attic into the useful space you dream of.

Look throughout the book for the "Tips" sections for other extra fun ideas, and check out the Resource Guide at the back which contains information about the designers of some of the spaces pictured.

Family Spaces

Family spaces are all-purpose, casual living spaces where the entire family can gather together to relax. They should be comfortable, practical additions that family members find themselves naturally gravitating toward during the evening. They should be open and inviting, yet intimate environments that encourage familial interaction. And basements and attics are prime locations for such needs.

Family spaces tend to be added to basements rather than attics for three reasons. First, the preferred size for a family room is 12 sq. ft. × 16 sq. ft., and basements are more likely to offer this much space. Secondly, basements tend to be darker than attics, an attribute conducive to watching movies and television. And finally, in more ambitious family spaces that include laundry rooms, bathrooms, or wet bars, it is usually easier to connect to the existing plumbing in basements.

Whether you're planning a modest remodel or something more lavish, take heart in the fact that, on average, over 80% of the costs of creating a new family space are recovered in an increase in your home's value.

This family room offers the best of two worlds: Comfy chairs with task lighting are oriented around a gas fireplace with a poured concrete hearth, oak mantle, and slate stone tile to create a peaceful space to read or talk. At the same time, the built-in maple cabinets house the entertainment system and media storage for a more lively setting.

Defining spaces without the use of walls is a common problem in basement remodels. The decorative slate tile accents not only repeat the materials found in the fireplace, they create a threshold that helps to distinguish between the game area and family room. The effect was achieved simply by furring out the wall with 2 × 4s. Other design strategies have also been employed to define space: The chandelier is the centerpiece of the game area and the lounge chair in foreground signals the beginning of the family room.

In family rooms with an entertainment center, creating appropriate storage for your audio/visual equipment and media is a major concern. At the low end there are ready-to-assemble (RTA) modular shelving systems or manufactured stand-alone units that can meet your basic needs. Many of these options, however, are disappointing to style-conscious consumers.

In this basement, a large custom built-in provides the perfect backdrop for this homeowner's entertainment center—keeping all wires out of sight and everything organized and within reach. The cabinet doors hiding the TV are on a pivot door slide so they can slide back out of the way. Together, the alder wainscot paneling, backlit storage cabinets, and array of wall sconces bring a richness and warmth to what used to be a dark lower level.

The rustic fireplace outfitted with old Chicago brick, a thick mantel, and alder paneling matching the built-in on the other wall, provides an alternative focal point to the room. The surround seating creates an intimate conversation or reading area when the television is behind closed doors.

Warm, neutral colors, faux finishes, and columns with molding styles matching the upstairs give a Mediterranean feel to this lower level. A beautifully curved, granite-top bar adds to the relaxed atmosphere. The bar has ample seating along the front for entertaining and is equipped with a full-sized refrigerator, microwave, dishwasher, oven, and cooktop.

This elegant family room is the perfect space to relax by the warmth of a fire or the glow of the big screen television. However, the real feature of this room is the full wall that has been crafted to create the feeling you're looking out onto the Italian countryside. The texture and appeal of the stone archway and pillars framing the painting is repeated in the tile of the fireplace surround, as well as in the arches and moldings at the entranceways.

While high gable ceilings can be dramatic, they pose a design challenge in that they can make a room feel impersonal and intimidating. Lowered ceilings can help create spaces that are more interesting and less imposing. Even the suggestion of a lowered ceiling with the use of chandeliers, beams, archways or even terraces can make a significant difference.

In this case, a seating area for the media room is tucked into a dormer and defined by the chandelier and the red oak hammer beam trusses. The spaces beneath a lowered feature will inevitably feel more private and comfortable than the rest of the attic.

The sitting area takes advantage of the morning and afternoon sun. From the two window seats, there is a great view of a creek or the neighbor's expansive gardens. Double-hung windows take full advantage of the tall end wall.

This beautiful attic is organized into two cozy sitting areas around a sizeable earth-tone fireplace near the center of the room. What might otherwise be an intimidating attic, due to the tall walls and vaulted ceiling, is divided into more manageable, human-scale spaces.

Every element is well considered to create the bright, contemporary look of this family space. The skylights are aligned with the windows below to create a measured sense of rhythm in the repetition of shapes. These simple, linear lines are then repeated in the modern Scandinavian furniture. The variegated oak floor presents the only "pattern" in the room. It creates a sense of warmth and continuity, whereas a floor in a solid color would be monotonous in this already understated space. A circular wall hanging presents an interesting contrast to the straight lines in the room.

A formerly long and narrow "bowling-alley" basement has been transformed into a vibrant lower level. The deep indigo blue of the bar and ceiling articulation (a 2"-deep decorative soffit) and rich red of the wall draw attention to these features because they are strong, saturated primary colors that play off one another well. The white ceiling, neutral carpeting and wall color, and blonde maple bar front and baseboards reflect light and make the space brighter.

Color Theory

There are several color harmonies derived from the color wheel that can make the process of choosing colors less perplexing.

- **Monochromatic** (single color) color combinations are variations in lightness and saturation of a single color. Their use creates a subtle reiteration of a color theme.
- **Analogous** colors (related hues—e.g., red and red-orange) are adjacent to one another on the color wheel. The use of these kindred colors creates a harmonious and unified effect.
- **Complementary** colors (opposite hues—e.g., red and green) are directly opposite one another on the color wheel. Their use creates an eye-popping color contrast.

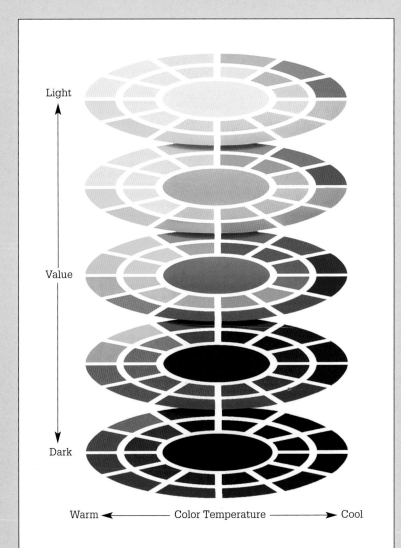

- **Split-complementary** colors are produced when a dominant color is opposite not its complementary color but the two colors adjacent to its complementary.

  Their use creates the same high contrast as complementaries, but without the same degree of intensity.

- **Triadic** colors are three equally spaced colors on the color wheel (making an equilateral triangle—e.g., purple, green, orange). Their use creates a harmonious color richness and strong visual contrast.

- Four colors are in a **Tetradic** or **Double Complementary** relation when two pairs of opposites on the color wheel create two sets of high-contrast colors (e.g., yellow-purple and orange-blue).

  When choosing paint, it is helpful to know that paint swatches are organized by three principles:

- The more black present in a color, the darker its **value**.

- The more white present in a color, the higher its **brightness**.

- The deeper, more vibrant a color is, the greater its **color saturation**.

The challenge posed by this basement was how to separate the laundry room on the right from the adjacent family room without closing off this already small space with more walls. The powder blue support post and Granny Smith apple green wall are adjacent on the color wheel and together create a split complementary color harmony with the opposing gypsy red of the shelving. This color relation helps to visually separate the family room, laundry room, and hallway and yet create a smooth transition from one to the next.

This storage unit separates the laundry area from the family room, while the open top throughout both rooms, allows air to circulate. The lemon yellow wall shared by both rooms, and the bead board ceiling that complements the shelving help to tie together the spaces.

Gypsy red and Spanish gold are "analogous colors"—they are adjacent on the color wheel. Therefore, they are useful for defining separate areas in this basement without fighting with each other visually. A built-in fireplace makes this a cozy place to watch television while folding laundry. An adjoining game room on the left and full bathroom on the right provide other diversions while waiting for laundry cycles to end.

Colors don't need to be bold to make a strong impression. The superabundance of white in this room—from the walls to the built-in cabinetry to the ceiling to the sofas—maintains a fresh and tidy appearance. And with most everything put away in closed storage, the white surfaces draw attention to carefully placed display items and the room's detailed woodwork.

This elegant screening room incorporates remote-control curtains for dramatic presentation. It's just like going to the theater, only the whole family gets free admission! The fastest growing trend in home design is the creation of a Home Theater. Advances in flat screens, projectors, speakers, and digital image and sound technology have made high-quality home theater environments affordable to more people than ever before.

Home Offices

Home offices are becoming a necessity for many of us: a 58% majority of all new homeowners request a home office. Some of us want a dedicated space just to manage daily tasks such as paying bills, surfing the Internet, and doing homework. However, there are a growing number of people who work income-generating jobs frequently or exclusively from their homes. In fact, nearly 20% of all working adults reported that they did at least some work at home as part of their primary job, according to the last survey conducted by the Bureau of Labor Statistics. And with computer technology growing by leaps and bounds daily, the number of telecommuters is only going to skyrocket.

Whatever your needs, basements and attics are great locations for a home office. They are generally quieter spaces than those on first or second floors, and their out-of-the-way location frees up traditionally defined living space in the rest of the house for everyday use. In order to be productive when working and relaxing when "at home," we need a sense of separation between our work-life and home-life. The act of descending or ascending the stairs to a basement or an attic affords us this sense of departure from our normal home space and becomes a kind of "commute." The transition can help us enter the mindset necessary for whatever set of tasks awaits us at the bottom or top of the landing.

At their best, home offices provide a home away from home, where work itself becomes a retreat. Home offices can do more than simply provide space for traditionally defined work activities. A unique design can create an environment that makes going to work a pleasure.

This homeowner has combined traditional cherry wood in furniture, flooring, and built-ins with a playful nautical theme to create a warm and inviting home office. Knotty pine-lined dormers suggest the shape of wooden-hulled ships pulling into port, and details such as the nautical-theme ceiling lighting fixture and the boat accent pieces are subtle touches that set the mood for the entire room. And of course, the nearby living room area provides space to socialize or take power naps for those much-needed breaks in the workday.

Many people find that an L-shaped desk arrangement is a convenient and efficient office layout.
A computer station as well as a writing and filing surface can both be accommodated with this arrangement.
You should be about an arm's length away from the monitor screen when you're sitting back in the chair.
Your eyes should be level with an imaginary line that is about 2" or 3" below the top of the monitor.

This gable extension provides a cozy, self-contained second workstation for the homeowner, who is a photographer, to sort through photographs. Just around the corner in the waiting room, an inexpensive bookcase was created with boards installed between the wall and a wood and plaster "chase" that hides a chimney and venting pipe, while the nearby narrow desk provides a great place to sort mail, jot notes, or set appointments—any of those small tasks that require space and time but that you wouldn't want taking over your main workspace.

Who says a basement has to be dark? With a little creativity a basement can be made into a comfortable home office. In this space a stationary window flanked by two spacious egress windows were carved out of the foundation wall, and a generously deep window well keeps natural light streaming inside. There is ample overhead and task lighting, as well as soft glowing pendant lights and the natural flickering light from the fireplace. The warm tones of the lights and wood materials in this room offsets the cold exposed pipes. This interesting floor was created with ½" birch plywood secured to the concrete floor through ¾" rigid insulation and a vapor barrier.

The small amount of floor space a spiral staircase occupies makes it a good choice for houses that don't have room to build a traditional access to the attic or basement. However, you'll need another entrance, perhaps on the exterior of the house, that is large enough to bring in office furniture or other large items.

The goal for any home office is to create an efficient, compact work area where everything you need is within reach. By utilizing every nook and cranny to its fullest potential, even an attic or basement with minimal floor space can be transformed into a fully equipped office with ample elbowroom.

Built-in storage and floor-to-ceiling bookshelves keep everything neatly put away and right at your fingertips. A TV screen tucked into a corner built-in provides entertainment or access to news and financials with a spin of the task chair. And with the monitor and wires tucked under the desk hutch with a pullout drawer for the keyboard, this office manages to achieve a fairly clean, minimalist look.

A shallow reach-in closet and small writing surface is all the space needed for a modest home office. The entire unit can be hidden from view with a pivoting door slide. The combination slide and hinge allows the door to open 90° and then slide or push back in along the inside edge of the cabinet, known as the "pocket."

A basement stairway produces a fabulous nook for a small office. A simple but functional workstation can be built with a few filing cabinets, a sheet of finished plywood, and a few stock or ready-to-assemble (RTA) cabinets for storage.

A humble home office can be organized under the slope of the gable ceiling at the top of the stairs of many attics. A simple 3' × 5' rug not only saves your floor from the wear and tear caused by a rolling office chair, but it helps to define the limits of the office area.

By installing a wall of windows and skylights on the southern corner of the house where the light is strongest, this home office takes best advantage of the available natural light and opens this small workspace to the world.

Hobby Spaces

The world seems to be shrinking. In this era of the information superhighway, we're more connected than ever before. But as technology devises new and numerous ways to keep us in contact and accessible to others, it becomes more difficult to find space for ourselves to pursue our individual interests.

Even a large house can feel small if we can't find a place to be alone when we need it. Research collected by the Hobby Association shows that 58% of us indulge in some form of art, craft, or hobby in the home, and the number is on the rise. Part of the increasing popularity of hobbies is that they give us license to retreat into a creative world we can call our own. And what better way to retreat into a personal creative realm than to carve out a dedicated space just for those inspired moments?

Whether it's scrapbooking or woodworking, candle making or wine tasting, model building or oil painting, this chapter illustrates how to find the perfect space for that hobby—and why the attic or basement are perfect places to consider.

Any art studio needs to have plenty of storage for supplies, good ventilation, and consistent lighting. This small attic area offers everything you need. The easel loosely defines the painting studio space against the rest of the attic. A standing screen or curtain could be installed to hide the workspace. There's plenty of space for oversized items.

Natural canvas, over-the-door shoe organizers are an easy and inexpensive way to keep your studio organized. They can be purchased for under $20 at discount or home stores and take up virtually no studio space at all. Paint a swatch of color across each pocket so that your color palette is easy to see at a glance, and then simply hang the organizer on a nearby door or from two heavy-duty picture hangers on a wall. You can also use the pockets to hold brushes, sponges, pens, pencils, erasers, and other supplies.

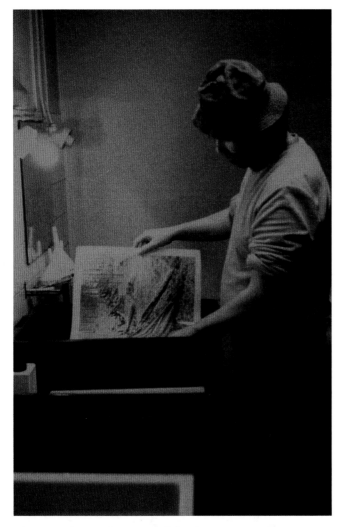

Photography requires a specialized space to work. Darkrooms include sealed doors to prevent light from entering, a ventilation system to displace chemical fumes, a sink, lots of shelving for storage, and a "safe light" or low intensity red light that illuminates your work but will not affect photographic paper.

(Above) This A-framed attic serves as a cozy get-away for relaxing and knitting. Knitting supplies can be stored in simple wicker baskets to add accents to the space, and a chest-of-drawers can be used to store additional needles, skeins of yarn, and patterns. Additionally, craft supplies can be easily transported if you need to open up the space to guests.

(Left) Sewing and quilting are activities that require space to spread out, as well as a lot of storage for the various supplies. Good lighting, smooth workspaces, and a comfortable place to sit are the prerequisites for any good sewing room. Inexpensive laminate floors provide the look of pricey redwood tongue-and-groove, and because they are perfectly smooth, it may be easier to find dropped needles. Full-spectrum overhead lighting illuminates the details, making it easier to locate seams and match up intricate fabric designs.

Good listening rooms often follow the "rule of eight"—that is, your speakers should stand 8 ft. apart with your listening position 8ft. back, forming a triangle.

To maintain good sound quality a listening room should contain a variety of materials so that it is neither too "hard" nor too "soft." Similarly, the ceiling and floor should be of opposite reflectivity. If the floor is absorptive (e.g., carpeting) the ceiling should be hard (e.g., drywall), and vice-versa. Also, arrange furniture, record racks, and other elements somewhat evenly around the room to break up the sound reflections caused by parallel planes.

A music listening room is separated from a home office by a striated glass wall. This gesture provides some privacy but maintains adequate light. However, flat glass surfaces are a no-no in listening rooms. Use either textured glass or cover the glass surfaces with a soft cloth shade or curtain. For the same reason, the wall behind the listener should generally be absorptive (e.g., a tapestry).

Libraries can provide the peace and quiet necessary for studying and practicing piano compositions. A cove or recessed ceiling is not only visually stimulating, but it is also an effective means of defining a room's space without walls.

Even the smallest attic space can become an elegant reading room. A few short bookcases, a combination of sunlight and task lighting, and a comfortable chair is all that's needed for a tranquil and pleasurable reading experience.

The dark and cool environment of basements provides optimal conditions for wine storage. Cellars usually stand at a steady 55°, the perfect temperature for wine, wine should be stored between 50° to 59° Fahrenheit. Wine storage areas should not reach 78°—the point at which it begins to uncork and "cook," resulting in a loss of quality. Humidity levels should also be controlled to stay between 50% and 70%. A heavy, solid-oak door helps to maintain a constant temperature and ensure that the room remains dark.

A workshop without adequate storage will go unused.
Wall space can be used to hang light and medium-duty tools on pegboard, plywood, slat-board, or a specially designed organizing system. Consider using a workbench that can be stored under other countertops or that can fold up against the wall when not in use.

Unfinished basement ceilings offer ample storage opportunity. For example, consider turning joist cavities into efficient storage cabinets. For instructions on this project and other organization ideas, refer to the *Black & Decker Complete Guide to Wood Storage Projects.*

Some storage items make contradictory demands—they need to be right at your fingertips, and out of the way. Wall hooks, clips, and forks attached to thermoplastic sliding tracks are flexible enough to display almost anything, and specific enough to be configured for unique needs.

A separate entrance to a basement workshop that is at least 36" wide allows you to accommodate larger projects and materials. It also can provide added ventilation—a basement workshop should have at least two windows for cross ventilation, as well as a fan and exhaust system. To help cut down on dust, install weather-stripping on all doors. Keep a broom, dustpan and wet/dry vacuum handy as workshops accumulate sawdust that is a fire hazard, an air-quality issue, and an unpleasant material to track upstairs.

Rec Rooms

In general, recreation rooms are spaces that can accommodate more boisterous activities than most family spaces can handle. "Rec" rooms, as they are called, are great spaces for kids to hang out and enjoy themselves with games, toys, and active play. In fact, these fun spaces give license to the kid in all of us to enjoy ourselves.

Rec rooms often begin as accidental repositories for all of the mismatched and inherited furniture and décor that just didn't look good in the rest of the house. And most often the only available space in the house for such items is found in unfinished basements and attics, where they can be tucked away from view. But rec rooms can be so much more, from game rooms to children's playrooms or home fitness centers and spas. With a little planning and forethought, a rec room can transcend its humble beginnings to become your favorite spot in the home.

A walkout basement can be the perfect party room for barbeques. It makes for easy access to the grill and keeps foot traffic from the outdoors out of the formal areas of the home. Bring in a pool table or other games to make the area even more fun. Comfortable seating near game tables is important as some games involve standing for long periods of time. And the nearby kitchenette is convenient for refueling between matches.

Game Rooms

Game rooms are a great way to decompress and can make social gatherings more lively and spirited. A billiards or ping-pong table, air hockey, pinball, arcade games, or home video games…whatever the space will hold, go for it. Game rooms are all about fun!

Game rooms typically require a lot of space, so they are usually located in basements as opposed to attics. Basements tend to offer the larger open floor spaces desirable for most game rooms, and unlike attics, most basements already have a solid floor suitable for heavy gaming tables and roughhousing. Basements are also cooler all year round, offering a more comfortable environment for active play.

Staggered game tables make the best use of space in this walkout basement. The game corner looks out to a backyard pond, creating a connection to the outdoors. The area also connects to an extended kitchen, living room, and eating area, making it part of a larger, sociable lower level.

A few nice built-in cabinets provide perfect toy storage in a child's playroom. And with a matching custom wood cover over electric baseboard radiators, the otherwise hot mechanical is safe for children to play around or on.

Playrooms

While playrooms are every child's dream, they can be a parent's delight as well. Converting a basement or attic into a child's play space can keep the noise and mayhem of play apart from the rest of the house.

Building a playroom is easy, but making the space safe, practical, and fun for kids takes some thoughtful planning. If you have small children, you may want the room within sight of a home office or family room, allowing you the freedom to work while you supervise the children. If the playroom must be in a remote location, you can install a home monitor or intercom system for communication between rooms.

Playrooms can be adapted easily into shared spaces so that caregivers can get some work done while keeping an eye on the children. Placing a computer workstation against an attic kneewall can create more play space in the center of the room and provide a spot for the children's own projects or homework.

(Above) Hideaways built to size. Houses are built proportionate to adult bodies, which can often leave little ones feeling disadvantaged. Inevitably, their favorite play spaces are the cozy nooks and crannies that allow them to feel completely in charge of their own environment.

(Right) An artist's painting on canvas covers a play space under the stairs. Inside the ship's galley, we find a clever play space, which is also accessible from the adjoining closet.

Stackable storage is a great way to make use of every unusually shaped nook and cranny in an attic or basement playroom. Open crates are an easy way to store toys. If it has a lid, cover or cabinet door to keep everything hidden away, so much the better.

Open shelves installed at the kneewall below skylights and roof windows provide the perfect place to store toys, books, and bins for crayons, stickers, or markers. Label bins to help children develop organization skills.

(Above) Studies show people tend to exercise more at home if the machines are in a specialized space and include a wide range of equipment. According to a recent survey, 29% of homeowners request a dedicated exercise room for their new home.

(Right) A variety of exercise equipment in a dedicated space can help you remain focused and inspired in your workout regimen. The full-wall mirrors help create the sense of more space and allow you to check on your form while exercising.

Exercise Rooms & Spas

If you are disciplined when it comes to fitness, all you need is a resistance band, jump rope, or yoga ball for stretching and strength training. But let's face it: most of us require some kind of motivation to get in shape. The first step to treating our bodies well is to have a dedicated fitness space, and it doesn't hurt to have some kind of "reward" in the area for relaxing after a strenuous workout, such as a sauna or spa.

Important things to keep in mind when adding an exercise room or spa to your home include: good lighting, adequate ventilation, and bright, cheery colors to keep you moving. And don't forget towel storage and a mini-fridge for water.

Adequate ventilation and cooling in an attic exercise room is a must. There should be at least two operable windows so you can create a cross-breeze in the space. Check with your builder to determine if your attic floor joists can support the weight of heavy machinery.

(Left) A home spa that is adequately separated from the day-to-day traffic paths of your home provides a splendid retreat without the stress of travel. Your unused basement or attic is the perfect place for such a destination. Dedicate your basement or attic as a place for relaxation and it will never sit dormant again.

(Below) Whether the focus is meditating, yoga, or cleansing baths followed by seaweed wraps and massages, basements are generally better for quiet retreats, in which dim lights are desired, and attics are often good for hot yoga or sunrise meditation.

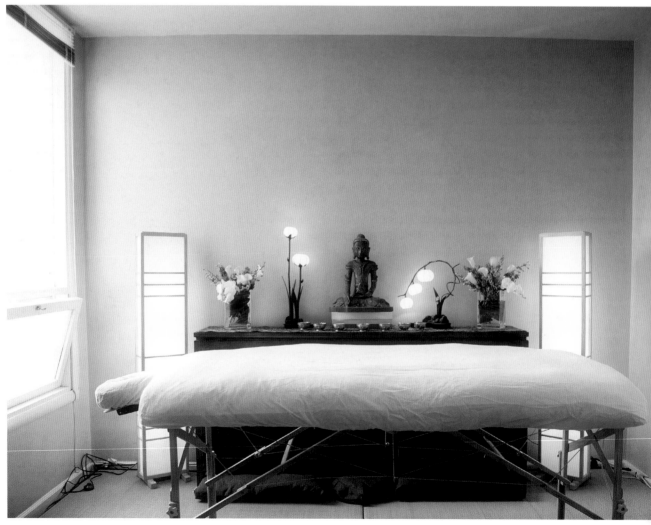

Steam rooms fit into the same amount of space as a standard tub or shower and provide humid heat as an alternative to the dry air of the sauna. Both saunas and steam rooms may relax stiff joints and muscles, cleanse your skin, eliminate toxins, raise your metabolism, and boost your immune system. Additionally, steam inhalation is an effective treatment in respiratory conditions, and through the use of essential oils in your steam spa's delivery system, you can pursue the benefits of aromatherapy, as well.

Bathrooms

Adding an extra bathroom is a luxury most home-owners dream about. Attics and basements are the perfect places to add a bathroom, especially if your family will be spending more time in these areas.

Begin the planning process by assessing the space you need. What size bathtub would you like—or is just a shower all that is needed? What size sink and toilet do you prefer? Do you need extra storage in the bathroom space? Next, consider the specifics of the space: Would you like non-skid floor surfaces, grab bars, and GFCI electrical circuit protectors? And, finally, plan the best location for the bathroom based on all of the above needs. Try to locate the bathroom near existing plumbing pipes to make the installation easier.

The following chapter will go into all the details for adding a bathroom to your attic or basement. There are also specific projects that follow, to make your entire process that much easier.

Light from the skylights is multiplied as it bounces between the skylights, window, ceiling, and walls. While installing a new bath can be a big project, it always pays off: the addition of a full bath adds about 24% to the resale value of your home.

A bath doesn't necessarily have to be tucked away in a corner. This contemporary master bath suite is located near the center of the attic and the bedroom occupies the cozy dormer behind it. A staggered wall offers privacy to those in either space without closing off the entry area. Raspberry accent tile dramatically sets off the bathtub from the vertical grain bamboo tub surround.

In some attics, the original floor structure may not be up to building code requirement for a finished space with a full tub. In that case, 2 × 10s must be installed between the old joists, often 2 × 6s, to reinforce the floor. And as with any attic bathroom, new plumbing waste pipes and vent pipes cannot simply be merged with those from the lower level; new pipes have to be installed to avoid creating a vacuum in the system.

In this sleek contemporary bathroom, every effort is made to allow unimpeded movement and open sightlines. The open window above the chrome and glass shower allows in additional natural light, makes the space feel less confined, and keeps moisture from getting trapped in the shower box. The sink and thin vanity shelf complement each other in shape, color, and design, helping to pull together the minimalist theme.

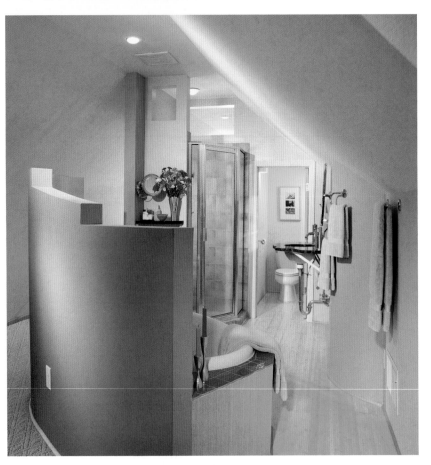

Having a bathing area and washing basin in a bedroom makes the morning or evening bathing ritual more convenient. You'll be surprised how nice it is to not have to bump into anyone in the hallway when you're half asleep. Tiling the tub surround and backsplash with an attractive mix of rusts, greens, and gold makes this room one-of-a-kind.

Bedrooms

Though we don't give it much thought, we spend as much as a third of our lives in our bedrooms. That's a lot of time. So it's well worth our while to create a bedroom environment that is comfortable and uniquely our own. Not only will we appreciate our homes more, we will be more likely to get the rest needed to tackle the other two-thirds of our lives.

A bedroom is a highly personal space. What makes a bedroom perfect for one person may not make it so for another. All great bedrooms, however, are alike in that they are designed to be retreats from the outside world. Ideally, they are in close proximity to a full bath, offer storage to keep the room uncluttered, are decorated with soothing colors, and include pleasant memorabilia associated with happy memories.

Whether you're considering a guest room, an additional bedroom for the kids, or a full master suite, basements and attics are the ideal location for a bedroom. Both spaces are set apart from the main living areas, so retiring for the night creates the sense that we are leaving our everyday cares behind, making it easier to relax, wind down, and get some rest.

For those of you blessed with a large attic, you can transform the space into a luxurious master suite complete with a bedroom, bathroom, and sitting area. The national average for a remodel of that magnitude is approximately $70,000; however, just over 80% of those costs are recouped at resale. The recoup value is even higher for more modest attic bedrooms.

An attic kneewall is the perfect solution for rooms with little to no storage space.

This master bedroom suite feels bright and open while remaining cozy. A vaulted ceiling like this one can be dramatic and intimidating, but the wood beams bring the room back to a human scale to maintain comfort.

(Left) This attic bedroom incorporates bright, warm colors and soft fabrics to generate feelings of warmth and comfort.

(Below) This attic achieves its sense of openness and sophistication by leaving everything from railing and plumbing to bricks and beams exposed. The built-in bookcases act as media storage, a safety rail and an elegant see-through wall.

Exposed brick can be a stylish accent in any room. Here it serves as an innovative backsplash for a bathroom vanity. Copper pipes are highlighted rather than hidden, contributing to the room's charm.

One way to carve a sleeping space from a larger room is with a room divider. This internally lit screen allows light to filter through and provides a bright, clean look. A Japanese screen or room divider can turn any area into two functional spaces while still allowing your attic or basement to feel airy and open.

Because darker colors feel "closer" than lighter colors, the sunflower yellow on the gable wall exaggerates the length of the room when juxtaposed with the poppy red of the ceilings. The rug runner contributes to the effect.

Combined with a periwinkle blue that is used in other areas of this bedroom suite, these colors are a "triadic" relation—three equally spaced colors on the color-wheel that provide a rich but harmonious visual contrast. The skylight opposite the bed offers additional natural light to make the colors stand out during the day and provides a view of the sky at night.

For a toned-down version of this design, choose a stand-out color for the headboard wall and paint the other three walls with a complementary relaxing, warm color.

This small attic has made great use of a limited space. There are no full walls to obstruct our view, but our eyes recognize two distinct layers: the narrow hallway in the foreground and the reading alcove beyond it. The green kneewall suggests where one space ends and the next begins. And when there are two or more layers in our field of vision, we perceive depth that may not actually exist, causing each space to appear larger than it actually is.

Strong colors applied with confidence and vivid imagination can make some people swear off of white walls for good. In this attic, a bouquet of rich, deep colors—periwinkle blue, apple green, sunset orange, and butter yellow—treat the eye to a tour around the color wheel. Even the flooring is incorporated into the inventive use of angles and colors: here Brazilian cherry and birch flooring are used to distinguish between the sitting area and bedroom.

With one sightline spanning the entire length of this space, the attic feels more spacious. The dramatic angles of the two openings into the bedroom inform you that you've entered a new place without the hindrance of doors.

(Above) Stackable storage blocks provide unique storage space, and the arrangement is limited only by your imagination.

(Right) Even if a child's basement bedroom doesn't have a window, it need not be dreary. Using bright colors and playful design can make a basement bedroom cozy and still fun to spend time in. In this room, a cheerful design is achieved with bright yellow paint on the walls, bright colored storage, and complementary bright fabrics. The non-linear shelf adds visual interest to an otherwise boxy room.

(Above) **An attic bedroom** with beds that resemble train berths is perfect for a visiting family. Separating beds with partition walls is an inexpensive way to give both kids and parents some privacy. Natural light from a skylight and a double-hung window makes it easier to rouse kids in the morning.

(Right) **Kids bedrooms with little or no natural light** can be brightened up with lively colors and spot lighting (in addition to overhead lighting).

With a little creativity, the awkward angles and recess of an attic can be the biggest asset in creating fun kids' bedrooms. In this aeronautically themed kid's bedroom, triangular shapes and angled lines dominate. They show up in rug patterns, window valances, and shelving built-ins. Mounted on the sloped walls, the mirrors produce a fun-house effect. And the sloped display shelving and platform bed of this biplane fit perfectly under the slope of the attic wall.

Suites

As the population ages, more and more families are looking for affordable alternatives to high-priced assisted-living facilities. An in-law suite, a second self-contained living quarter in a single-family home, is becoming an increasingly common solution.

Also called "second suites," "accessory apartments," or "granny flats," in-law suites are often subject to zoning bylaws designed to curtail their use as retail rentals for non-family members. Some jurisdictions prohibit a single-family home from having two full kitchens, while others forbid a suite from having a separate entrance. However, in many areas, bylaws are changing to accommodate the growing desire for extended families to live together under one roof. These jurisdictions may simply require that there is a direct access from the main dwelling to the in-law suite and may periodically ask for verification that there is a family member living in the space.

Zoning issues aside, a basement or attic is the ideal location for an in-law suite. Because they are apart of the house structure, and yet set apart from the main living area, these spaces strike the perfect balance between the occupant's need for independence and for close contact with the family when desired.

Murphy beds, or wall beds, are stored vertically inside a wall cabinet or cavity and fold downward when needed. They use specially designed mattresses weighted for the spring-balanced Murphy frame and, when stored vertically, occupy as little as 16 in. of floor space. Initial installation of many models takes from 4 to 6 hours to complete, and most manufacturers recommend that they be professionally installed. They are perfect for rooms with limited space.

Large pass-throughs to the living area and to a small but fully functional kitchenette allow the occupant greater independence. These considerations may not be important to short-term guests, but for a full-time aging relative, they are critical in fostering a relationship of equality and respect.

This plush, Tuscan-inspired in-law suite was designed for young adults visiting from school. There is a home theater and bar with tasting table to use for entertaining guests as well.

Rather than lining up furniture along the walls, "floating" furnishings in the middle of the room into close-knit groupings no more than 8 ft. apart routes traffic around a sitting area rather than through it to create intimate conversation areas for family or guests.

Design Tips

- Soundproof the walls and floors between your in-law suite and your home as much as possible. Use sound insulation in the walls, install solid-core rather than hollow-core doors, and if possible, install the sheetrock on "sound channels."

- Plan for future health concerns. Slightly wider doors (2', 10" in residences are fine) and larger bathrooms allow more space for maneuvering walkers or wheelchairs. Additionally, low-barrier shower units and grab-bars around elongated toilets will extend the time your in-laws can stay in the unit.

- Design in a kitchenette if at all possible, even if it's only a microwave and a refrigerator. Your in-laws will feel more independent if they can make their own coffee and breakfast in the morning without having to come into the main kitchen.

- Install a separate entrance to the in-law suite if at all possible so your in-laws can have their privacy, their guests can come and go without disturbing your family, and so everyone can feel more independent.

- Provide windows to the street if at all possible. Privacy and views to nature are fine, but human beings are social creatures and love to see who's coming and going.

- Above all, plan now for how the in-law space could be used in the future. Can it be converted into a master bedroom suite? Would it function well as a home office? Could it be rented out as an apartment?

(Above) Looking out from the cherry wood kitchenette, the molded ceiling and wooden beams add a touch of elegance to this lower level that is usually reserved for upper floors. While a Tudor-style light fixture and antique furnishings echo this formal look, curved arches in the doorway and bookshelves lend a softer feel to a room also used for recreational purposes.

A storage wall adds visual depth to a space and gives live-in family members a place to put objects brought from their homes that are important to them.

(Right) This quaint suite will surely keep guests around—all the essentials are packed within this small, cozy space: a kitchenette, table, bed, and closet. The window allows natural light in, preventing a claustrophobic feel. The kitchenette can be completely concealed with a pull door, transforming the dining area into an office space or living room.

Dormers can provide the added space needed to create the perfect nook. Here, a thick leather couch, flatscreen TV, and plenty of natural light from a transom window make this an inviting area for hanging out. Directly behind the couch, a desk takes advantage of the remaining space, providing a perch for doing homework or paying bills.

A small kitchen with microwave and sink is perfect for quick snacks and instant meals. A crockpot is a simple addition to a small kitchen and drastically increases meal planning options.

This minimalist, contemporary suite provides a clean and sophisticated atmosphere. Instead of shying away from the coolness associated with basements, this space plays upon the theme with calming blues and grays.

Projects: Getting Started

Although many attics and basements are good candidates for finishing, not all are suitable. Some spaces are simply too small or have very low ceilings or problems like flooding that make the investment too risky. If you've been thinking about remodeling, chances are the space is usable, but it could require some expensive preparation work to ensure safety and structural integrity over time. Of course, it's best to know this early in the process. Therefore, the first step is to evaluate the space to find out what you have to work with, what changes are necessary, and how much everything will cost.

The primary gauge by which to measure your attic or basement is the local building code. This code describes all the requirements for livable spaces in your area, and it governs every aspect of your project. There are code specifications for everything from minimum headroom to how many electrical receptacles you'll need in your new family room. For personal reference, you can probably find a copy of the building code at a local library, but for the most part, you'll learn about the requirements from the officials at the building department. They can also warn you about problems specific to your area, such as a high water table or expansive soil.

This section shows you the basic elements to look for as you evaluate your basement or attic. Much of this you can check out yourself; other matters may require professional examination. If your attic or basement passes your evaluation, hire an architect, engineer, or building contractor to have a look at the space and the elements that will be affected by the project. You can also use your home's original blueprints to learn about the basic structure of the house and locate mechanical rough-ins without cutting holes in the walls. If you don't have blueprints, contact your home's builder or the city office to get a copy of them.

When you've finished the evaluation stage and are ready to start remodeling, take some time to plan the project and draft a construction schedule. This step includes designing the space, getting the building permits, and establishing an order for all of the construction that follows. It's a challenging part of the remodeling process, but creating an effective plan is essential to a successful project.

Evaluating Your Attic

Start your attic evaluation with a quick framing inspection. If the roof is framed with rafters, you can continue to the next test. If it's built with trusses, however, consider remodeling your basement instead. The problem is that the internal supports in trusses leave too little space to work with, and trusses cannot be altered.

The next step is to check for headroom and overall floor space. Most building codes call for 7½ ft. of headroom over 50% of the "usable" floor space, which is defined as any space with a ceiling height of at least 5 ft. Remember that these minimums apply to the finished space—after the flooring and ceiling surfaces are installed. Other things can affect headroom, as well, such as reinforcing the floor frame, and increasing rafter depth for strength or insulation.

You may also find various supports in your attic that are there to strengthen your roof but may limit your space. *Collar* ties are horizontal boards that join two rafters together in the upper third of the rafter span. They prevent rafter uplift in high winds. Often collar ties can be moved up a few inches but cannot be removed. *Rafter* ties join rafters in the lower third of their span to prevent spreading. In most attics, the ceiling or floor joists serve as rafter ties. *Purlins*

Rafter framing creates open space in an attic because the rafters carry most of the roof's weight.

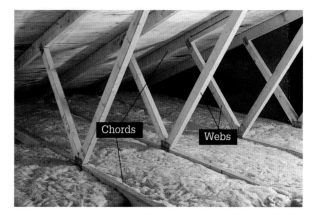

Trusses are made of interconnected cords and webs, which close off most of the attic space.

are horizontal boards that run at right angles to the rafters and are supported by struts. These systems shorten the rafter span, allowing the use of smaller lumber for the rafters. You may be allowed to substitute kneewalls for purlins and struts. If you'll need to have any support system altered or moved, consult an architect or engineer.

The rafters themselves also need careful examination. Inspect them for signs of stress or damage, such as cracks, sagging, and insect infestation. Look for dark areas indicating roof leaks. If you find leaks or you know your roofing is past its useful life, have it repaired or replaced before you start the finishing process. And even if the rafters appear healthy, they may be too small to support the added weight of

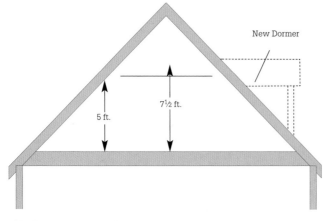

Habitable rooms must be at least 70 sq. ft. total and measure at least 7 ft. in any one direction. To meet headroom requirements, 50% of the usable floor space must have a ceiling height of 7½ ft.

You can add to your floor space and headroom by adding protruding windows called *dormers*. In addition to space, dormers add light and ventilation to your attic.

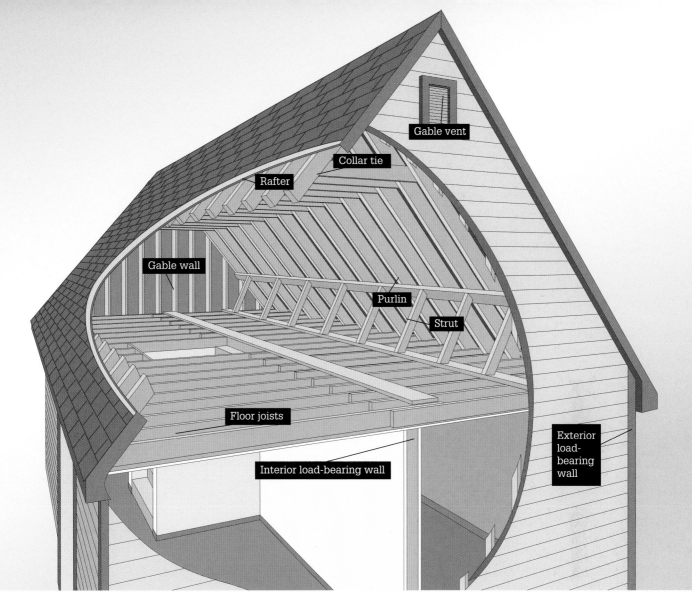

Gable vent

Collar tie

Rafter

Gable wall

Purlin

Strut

Floor joists

Interior load-bearing wall

Exterior load-bearing wall

finish materials. Small rafters can also be a problem if they don't provide enough room for adequate insulation.

At this point, it's a good idea to have a professional check the structural parts of your attic, including the rafters and everything from the floor down. In some cases, finishing an attic is like adding a story to your home, which means that the structure must have adequate support for the new space. Attic floors are often built as ceiling frames for the level below and are not intended to support living space. Floors can be strengthened with additional joists, known as *sister* joists or with new joists installed between the existing ones.

Support for the attic floor is provided by the load-bearing walls below and, ultimately, by the foundation. If these elements can't support the finished attic, they'll need to be reinforced. This may be as simple as strengthening the walls with plywood panels or as complicated as adding support posts and beams or reinforcing the foundation.

In addition to these structural matters, there are a few general code requirements you should keep in mind as you inspect your attic. If you plan to add a bedroom, it will need at least one exit to the outside. This can be a door leading to an outside stairwell or an egress window. Most codes also have minimum requirements for ventilation and natural light, which means you may have to add windows or skylights.

One of the largest expenses of finishing an attic is in providing access: You'll need a permanent stairway at least 36" wide, with room for a 36" landing at the top and bottom. This is an important planning issue because adding a stairway affects the layout and traffic patterns of the attic as well as the floor below.

Finally, take an inventory of existing mechanicals in your attic. While plumbing and wiring runs can be moved relatively easily, other features, such as chimneys, must be incorporated into your plans. This is a good time to have your chimney inspected by a fire official and to obtain the building code specifications for framing around chimneys.

Evaluating Your Basement

The two things that put an end to most basement finishing plans are inadequate headroom and moisture. Begin your evaluation by measuring from the basement floor to the bottom of the floor joists above. Most building codes require habitable rooms to have a finished ceiling height of 7½ ft., measured from the finished floor to the lowest part of the finished ceiling. However, obstructions, such as beams, soffits, and pipes, (spaced at least 4 ft. on center) usually can hang down 6" below that height. Hallways and bathrooms typically need at least 7-ft. ceilings.

While it's impractical to add headroom in a basement, there are some ways of working around the requirements. Ducts and pipes often can be moved, and beams and other obstructions can be incorporated into walls or hidden in closets or other uninhabitable spaces. Also, some codes permit lower ceiling heights in rooms with specific purposes, such as recreation rooms. If headroom is a problem, talk to the local building department before you dash your dreams.

If your basement passes the headroom test, you can move on to the next issue: moisture. For a full discussion on this critical matter, see *Dealing with Basement Moisture,* on page 92. Be aware that moisture problems must be corrected before you start the finishing process.

A well-built basement is structurally sound and provides plenty of support for finished space, but before you cover up the walls, floor, and ceiling, check for potential problems. Inspect the masonry carefully. Large cracks may indicate shifting of the soil around the foundation; severely bowed or out-of-plumb walls may be structurally unsound. Small cracks usually cause moisture problems rather than structural woes, but they should be sealed to prevent further cracking. Contact an engineer or foundation contractor for help with foundation problems. If you have an older home, you may find sagging floor joists overhead or rotted wood posts or beams; any defective wood framing will have to be reinforced or replaced.

Your basement's mechanicals are another important consideration. The locations of water heaters, pipes, wiring, circuit boxes, furnaces, and ductwork can have a significant impact on the cost and difficulty of your project. Can you plan around components, or will they have to be moved? Is there enough headroom to install a suspended ceiling so mechanicals can remain accessible? Or, will you have to reroute pipes and ducts to increase headroom? Electricians and HVAC contractors can assess your systems and suggest modifications.

Aside from being dark and scary places, unfinished basements often harbor toxic elements. One of the most common is *radon,* a naturally occurring radioactive gas that is odorless and colorless. It's believed that prolonged exposure to high levels of radon can cause lung cancer. The Environmental Protection Agency has free publications to help you test for radon and take steps to reduce the levels in your house. For starters, you can perform a "short-term" test using a kit from a hardware store or home center. Look for the phrase "Meets EPA requirements" to ensure the test kit is accurate. Keep in mind that short-term tests are not as

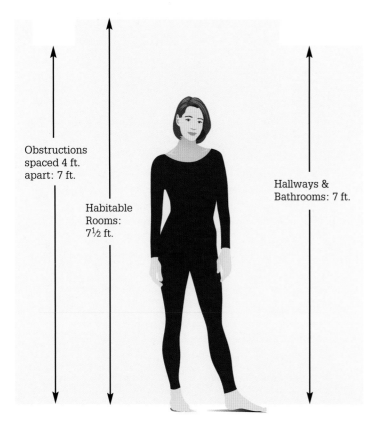

Obstructions spaced 4 ft. apart: 7 ft.

Habitable Rooms: 7½ ft.

Hallways & Bathrooms: 7 ft.

Basement headroom is often limited by beams, ducts, pipes, and other elements. Typical minimums for ceiling height are shown here: 7½ ft. for habitable rooms; 7 ft. for bathrooms and hallways; 7 ft. for obstructions spaced no less than 4 ft. apart.

Tips for Evaluating Your Basement

Rerouting service lines and mechanicals adds quickly to the expense of a project, so consider your options carefully.

Weakened or undersized joists and other framing members must be reinforced or replaced.

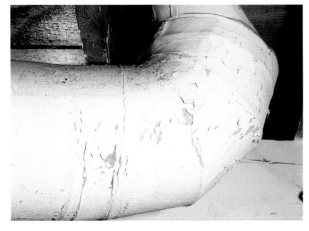

Old insulation containing asbestos poses a serious health risk if it is deteriorating or is disturbed.

Minor cracks such as these in masonry walls and floors usually can be sealed and forgotten, while severe cracking may indicate serious structural problems.

conclusive as professional, long-term tests. If your test reveals high levels of radon, contact a radon specialist.

Another basement hazard is insulation containing asbestos, which was commonly used in older homes for insulating ductwork and heating pipes. In most cases, this insulation can be left alone provided it's in good condition and is protected from damage. If you fear the insulation in your basement poses a hazard, contact an asbestos abatement contractor to have it evaluated or safely removed.

Also check the local codes for exits from finished basements—most codes require two. The stairway commonly serves as one exit, while the other can be a door to the outside, an egress window, or a code-compliant *bulkhead* (an exterior stairway with cellar doors). Each bedroom will also need an egress window or door for escape.

Stairways must also meet local code specifications. If yours doesn't, you'll probably have to hire someone to rebuild it. See page 95 for an overview of typical staircase requirements.

As a final note, if you're planning to finish the basement in a new house, ask the builder how long you should wait before starting the project. Poured concrete walls and floors need time to dry out before they can be covered. Depending on where you live, you may be advised to wait up to two years, just to be safe.

Dealing with Basement Moisture

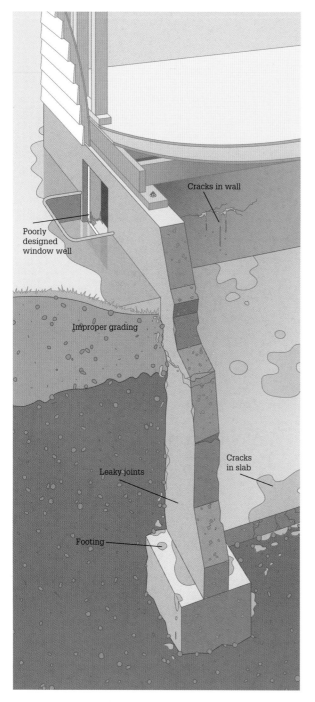

Basement moisture can destroy your efforts to create functional living space. Over time, even small amounts of moisture can rot framing, turn wallboard to mush, and promote the growth of mold and mildew. Fortunately, most moisture problems can be resolved, but any measures you take must prove effective before you proceed with your project. Ensuring your basement will stay dry throughout the seasons may take a year or more, but considering the time and money involved, it's worth the delay.

Basement moisture appears in two forms: condensation and seepage. Condensation comes from airborne water vapor that turns to water when it contacts cold surfaces. Vapor sources include humid outdoor air, poorly ventilated appliances, damp walls, and water released from concrete. Seepage is water that enters the basement by infiltrating cracks in the foundation or by leeching through masonry. Often caused by ineffective exterior drainage, seepage comes from rain or groundwater that collects around the foundation or from a rising water table.

If you have a wet basement, look for evidence of moisture problems. Typical signs include peeling paint, white residue on masonry, mildew stains, sweaty windows and pipes, rusted appliance feet, rotted wood near the floor, buckled floor tile, and strong mildew odor.

To test for condensation and seepage, lay a square of plastic or aluminum foil on the floor and another on an exterior foundation wall. Tape down all four sides of each. Check the squares after two days. If moisture has formed on top of a square, you probably have a condensation problem; moisture on the underside indicates seepage.

To reduce condensation, run a dehumidifier in the basement. Insulate cold-water pipes to prevent condensate drippage, and make sure your dryer and other appliances have vents running to the outside. Central A/C service in the basement can help reduce vapor during warm, humid months.

Crawlspaces can also promote condensation, as warm, moist air enters through vents and meets cooler interior air. Crawlspace ventilation is a source of ongoing debate, and there's no universal method that applies to all climates. It's best to ask the local building department for advice on this matter.

Solutions for preventing seepage range from simple do-it-yourself projects to expensive professional jobs requiring excavation and foundation work.

Common causes of basement moisture include improper grading around the foundation, inadequate or faulty gutter systems, humidity and condensation, cracks in foundation walls, leaky joints between structural elements, and poorly designed window wells. More extensive problems include large cracks in the foundation, damaged or missing drain tiles, a high water table, or the presence of underground streams. Often, a combination of factors is at fault.

Test for condensation and seepage by taping a square of aluminum foil to the floor and a wall. Moisture on top of the foil indicates condensation; moisture underneath reveals seepage.

Since it's often difficult to determine the source of seeping water, it makes sense to try some common cures before calling in professional help.

Begin by checking your yard's grade. The first 6 ft. of ground around the foundation should slope away at a rate of 1" per foot and at least ¾" per foot beyond that. Use a level, long board and tape measure to check the grade. Build up the ground around the foundation to improve drainage.

Next, inspect your downspouts and gutters. Give the gutters a thorough cleaning, and patch any holes. Make sure the gutters slope toward the downspouts at about ¹⁄₁₆" per foot. And most important, add downspout extensions and splashblocks to keep roof runoff at least 8 ft. away from the foundation.

Window wells also allow water into a basement. Covering them with removable plastic is the easiest way to keep them dry. If you prefer to leave wells uncovered, add a gravel layer and a drain to the bottom of the well. Clean the well regularly to remove moisture-heavy debris.

To further help stop seepage, patch cracks in the foundation walls and floors. Use waterproof masonry sealant for cracks under ¼" wide, and use hydraulic cement for larger cracks. Whole-wall interior coatings, such as masonry waterproofer, may also help reduce basement moisture. However, be aware that while sealing the foundation from the inside can help block occasional and light moisture, it will not solve serious moisture problems.

If these simple measures don't correct your moisture problems, you must consider more extensive action. Serious water problems are typically handled by footing drains or sump systems. Footing drains are

installed around the foundation's perimeter, near the footing, and they drain out to a distant area of the yard. These usually work in conjunction with waterproof coatings on the foundation walls. Sump systems use an interior under-slab drain pipe to collect water in a pit, and water is sent outside by an electric sump pump.

Find out if your house has one of these systems in place. It may be that your footing drain pipes are clogged with silt or have been damaged by tree roots. If you have a sump pit in your basement floor but no pump or discharge pipe in place, you may need to install a pump and drain lines. (There may be regulations about where the sump pump drains.)

Installing a new drainage system is expensive and must be done properly. Adding a sump system involves breaking up the concrete floor along the basement's perimeter, digging a trench, and laying a perforated drainpipe in a bed of gravel. After the sump pit is installed, the floor is patched with new concrete. Installing a footing drain is far more complicated. This involves digging out the foundation, installing gravel and drainpipe, and waterproofing the foundation walls. A footing drain is considered a last-resort measure.

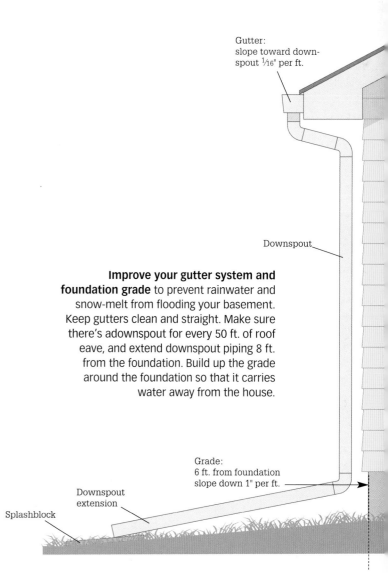

Gutter:
slope toward downspout ¹⁄₁₆" per ft.

Downspout

Improve your gutter system and foundation grade to prevent rainwater and snow-melt from flooding your basement. Keep gutters clean and straight. Make sure there's a downspout for every 50 ft. of roof eave, and extend downspout piping 8 ft. from the foundation. Build up the grade around the foundation so that it carries water away from the house.

Grade:
6 ft. from foundation slope down 1" per ft.

Downspout extension

Splashblock

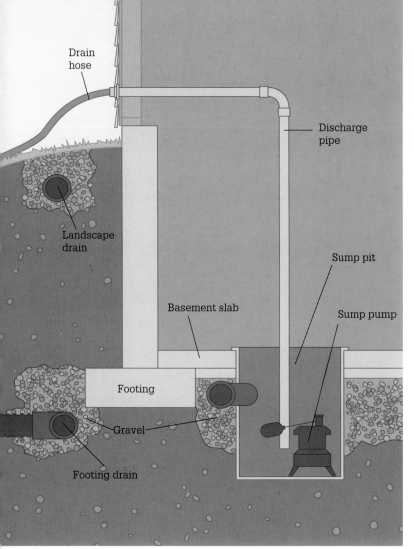

Drain hose

Discharge pipe

Landscape drain

Sump pit

Basement slab

Sump pump

Footing

Gravel

Footing drain

Foundation drainage systems are designed to remove water that pools around footings. Footing drains collect water from outside the footing and carry it out to daylight. Sump systems collect water underneath the basement floor and divert it into a pit. As the pit fills, a sump pump sends the water outside. Landscape drains remove water near the surface.

Find out if your house has one of these systems in place. It may be that your footing drain pipes are clogged with silt or have been damaged by tree roots. If you have a sump pit in your basement floor, but no pump or discharge pipe in place, you may need to install a pump and drain lines. (Be aware that there may be regulations about where the sump pump drains.)

Installing a new drainage system is expensive and must be done properly. Adding a sump system involves breaking up the concrete floor along the basement's perimeter, digging a trench, and laying a perforated drain pipe in a bed of gravel. After the sump pit is installed, the floor is patched with new concrete. Installing a footing drain is far more complicated. This involves digging out the foundation, installing gravel and drain pipe, and waterproofing the foundation walls. Thus, a footing drain is typically considered a last-resort measure.

Before you hire someone to install a drainage system, do some homework. Learn about the procedure the contractor has planned, and find out if it has been successful with other homes in your area. Check the contractor's references, and don't be afraid to get a second or third opinion before deciding.

To help stop seepage from inside the basement, patch cracks in the foundation walls and floors. Use waterproof masonry sealant for cracks under ¼" wide, and use hydraulic cement for larger cracks. Whole-wall interior coatings, such as masonry waterproofer, may also help reduce basement moisture. However, be aware that while sealing the foundation from the inside can help block occasional and light moisture, it will not solve serious moisture problems, regardless of the manufacturer's claims.

If these simple measures don't correct your moisture problems, you must consider more extensive action. Serious water problems are typically handled by footing drains or sump systems. Footing drains are installed around the foundation's perimeter, near the footing, and they drain out to a distant area of the yard. These usually work in conjunction with waterproof coatings on the foundation walls. Sump systems use an interior under-slab drain pipe to collect water in a pit. From there, the water is sent outside by an electric sump pump.

Fill cracks in the foundation with masonry waterproofer or hydraulic cement. This helps reduce minor seepage and prevents further cracking.

Stairways

An attic or basement finishing project requires safe access—both during the construction phase and after completion. And while you may have an existing stairway that's seen plenty of use, chances are it doesn't meet building code requirements for finished spaces. If there is no stairway, you'll need to plan carefully to find the best location for a new one. And because stairways must tie into the house framing, it's best to have this work done before anything else.

According to most building codes, basement and attic stairways must be at least 36" wide, with a minimum of 6 ft., 8" of headroom. Each step may have a maximum riser height of $7\frac{3}{4}$" and a minimum tread depth of 10". In addition, stairwells are required to have a 34"- to 38"-high handrail on at least one side, and a minimum 36"-deep landing at both the top and bottom of the stairs. And all stairways must be illuminated.

When evaluating your stairway, take into account your finishing plans. Steps must be as uniform as possible, with no more than a $\frac{3}{8}$" variance in riser height. Thick tile or a basement subfloor that runs up to the first step will shorten the height of the first

riser, creating an unsafe situation that doesn't meet code. You can adjust a new staircase to compensate for this, but an existing one doesn't offer such flexibility.

To plan a new staircase, consider how it will affect the surrounding spaces, as well as the traffic patterns, on both floors. The type of staircase you choose and where you put it will largely be determined by the available floor space. A standard straight-run stairway will occupy almost 50 sq. ft. of floor space on the lower level and 35 to 40 sq. ft. on the upper level. L- and U-shape stairways make 90° and 180° turns, respectively, allowing them to fit into smaller areas. *Winders* are L-shape stairs that make the turn with wedge-shape steps rather than a square platform. These allow a steeper rise in a confined area.

A spiral staircase offers a space-saving alternative for attic access. Spirals are available in stock sizes, or you can have them custom-built. However, spirals are not for everyone. They can be difficult to use for older people and young children, and some building codes limit their use as primary staircases.

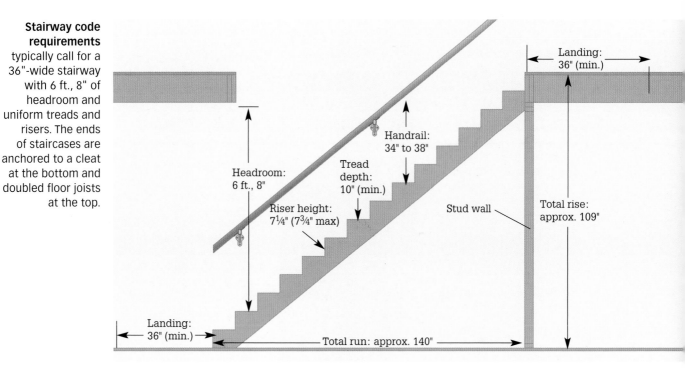

Stairway code requirements typically call for a 36"-wide stairway with 6 ft., 8" of headroom and uniform treads and risers. The ends of staircases are anchored to a cleat at the bottom and doubled floor joists at the top.

Landing: 36" (min.)

Headroom: 6 ft., 8"

Handrail: 34" to 38"

Tread depth: 10" (min.)

Riser height: 7¼" (7¾" max)

Stud wall

Total rise: approx. 109"

Landing: 36" (min.)

Total run: approx. 140"

Planning the Project

After you've evaluated your basement or attic and have determined that the space is usable, the next step is to plan the construction project. Having a complete construction plan enables you to view the entire project at a glance. It helps you identify potential problems, provides a sense of the time involved, and establishes a logical order of steps. Without a construction plan, it's easier to make costly errors, like closing up a wall with wallboard before the rough-ins are inspected.

It may help your planning to start with the end-results and work backwards. Think about each room in its finished state and consider how you will use it. What will you need for lighting? How will the space be heated? Is an emergency exit required? Defining the finished product now will also help you sort out the details, such as whether the cabinets should be installed before or after the flooring.

The general steps shown here follow a typical construction sequence. Your plan may differ at several points, but thinking through each of these steps will help you create a complete schedule.

Design the space. This is when you put your dreams to the test. Take measurements, make sketches, and test different layouts—find out what works and what doesn't. Consider all the necessary elements, such as headroom, lighting, mechanicals, and make sure everything adheres to local building codes. Determine whether mechanicals must be relocated.

Contact the building department. To avoid any unpleasant—and expensive—surprises, discuss your project with a building official. Find out what codes apply in your area and what you'll need to obtain the applicable permits. Explain how much of the work you plan to do yourself. (In some states, plumbing, electrical, and HVAC work must be done by licensed professionals.) Also determine what types of drawings you'll need to get permits.

Draw floor plans. Most attic and basement remodels can follow a simple set of plans that you can draw yourself. Start with copies of the original house plans, or simply measure the space and transfer the dimensions to graph paper. Basic floor plans should include dimensions of rooms, doors, and windows; all plumbing fixtures and HVAC equipment; electrical fixtures, receptacles, and switches; and closets, counters, and other built-in features. If you want professional help for this step, contact an architect, interior designer, remodeling contractor, or a design specialist at a home center.

Hire contractors. If you're getting help with your project, it's best to find and hire the contractors early in the process, as their schedules will affect yours. You may also need to have certain contractors pull their own permits at the building department. To avoid problems, make sure all of the contractors know exactly what work they are being hired to do and what work you will be doing yourself. Always check contractors' references and make sure they're licensed and insured before hiring them.

Get the permits.
Take your drawings, notes, and any required documents down to the building department, and obtain the permits for your project. Find out what work needs to be inspected and when to call for inspections. This is a critical step, as the permit process is required by law. Failure to get permits and the required inspections can make it difficult to sell your house and can negate your claim in insurance matters.

Make major structural & mechanical changes.
Prepare the space for finishing by completing structural work and building new stairs, if necessary. Move mechanical elements and re-route major service lines. Also complete any rough-ins that must happen before the framing goes up, such as adding ducts, installing under-floor drains, and replacing old plumbing.

Frame the rooms.
Build the floors, walls, and ceilings that establish your new rooms. In most cases, the floor will come first; however, you may want to rough-in service lines and insulate for soundproofing before installing the subfloor. Next come the walls. Cover foundation walls, and build partition walls and kneewalls. Build the rough openings for windows and doors. Enlarge existing basement window openings or cut new ones for egress windows. Install the windows.

Complete the rough-ins.
Run DWV (drain, waste, and vent) and water and gas supply pipes. Install electrical boxes, and run the wiring. Install additional wiring, such as speaker wire and cables for phones, televisions, intercoms, and Internet access. Complete the HVAC rough-ins. Build soffits to enclose new service lines. For future reference, it's a good idea to take photographs or jot down some measurements of pipe and wire locations.

Insulate. Insulate the walls, ceilings, and pipes for weatherizing and soundproofing. Install fiberglass insulation used as fireblocking. Make sure protector plates for pipes and wires running through framing are in place. Add vapor barriers as required by local code.

Finish the walls & ceilings. Make sure everything is in place before you cover up the framing. If you're installing wallboard, do the ceilings first, then the walls. Tape and finish the wallboard. Install other finish treatments. Texture, prime, and paint the wallboard when it's most convenient. If installing suspended ceilings, do so after finishing the walls.

Add the finishing touches. Complete the general finish carpentry, such as installing doors, moldings and other woodwork, cabinets, and built-in shelving, and lay the floor coverings. The best order for these tasks will depend on the materials you're using and the desired decorative effects.

Make the final connections. Install the plumbing fixtures, and complete the drain and supply hook-ups. Make electrical connections, and install all fixtures, devices, and appliances. You're finished with the construction when you get the final inspection and approval from the building inspector.

Basic Framing

Framing includes all the wood structures and surfaces that make up the rooms, hide the mechanicals, and enclose the unlivable spaces in your basement or attic. And, like all major construction elements, framing requires careful planning.

The first step is creating the layout of the finished space and making some drawings to work from. Some wall locations will be determined by existing elements, such as plumbing pipes, while others can follow a more aesthetic logic. Once your space is mapped out, you can begin work on the floor. Attic floors often need reinforcing to support the new living space. Basement floors usually need only a little patching or smoothing out, but you may decide to build a shallow wood subfloor over the concrete.

The types of walls you build will depend on the existing elements. You can cover basement foundation walls with furring strips attached to the masonry or with free-standing stud walls. In attics, short kneewalls define the sides of the space, and partition walls with angled top plates divide the areas in between. If you want a flat ceiling in your attic, frame it in before you build the partition walls. Door frames are easy to build into new interior walls, while window frames require modifying the existing framing or masonry. If your plans include a new skylight, see page 206.

Before you start framing, check with the building department to find out where you'll need fireblocking. Fireblocking is typically solid framing lumber or unfaced fiberglass insulation that's nailed or stuffed into framing cavities. It slows the spread of fire from one floor to another. Most building codes require fireblocking in framed walls, vertical chases, and soffits. Also, make sure you haven't forgotten any preliminary rough-ins—like adding a new furnace duct—that will be much more difficult with new walls in place.

Use graph paper to sketch your wall layouts. Scale your floor plan (aerial view) drawings at ¼" equals 1 ft. For elevation drawings (wall details as viewed from the side), use a scale of ½" equals 1 ft.

Draw layouts onto your basement floor with sidewalk chalk. Use different colors to represent elements other than walls, such as doors, windows, and ceiling soffits. Remove the chalk with a damp rag.

Planning the Framing

Use walls to define your new spaces. Walls can create quiet private retreats or comfortable bathrooms or serve as barriers between formal living areas and dusty, unfinished storage spaces. To determine where your walls should go, start with a thorough investigation of the unfinished space. All obstacles, such as mechanical systems, service lines, floor drains, support columns, chimneys, and roof framing, must be considered. As you work with different layouts, think about which of these elements can be enclosed by walls, which can be hidden within a wall or concealed by a soffit or chase, and which, if any, can be moved.

One technique to help you get started is to draw full-scale "walls" onto your basement floor, using children's sidewalk chalk (on wood attic floors, use wide masking tape instead of chalk). This can help you visualize the planned spaces and give you a better sense of room sizes. Complete the proposed layout in chalk, then walk through the rooms to test the traffic patterns. As you plan your rooms, keep in mind that most building codes require habitable

rooms to have at least 70 sq. ft. of floor space and measure a minimum of 7 ft. in any direction.

The next step is to draw floor plans. This doesn't require drafting skills—just a tape measure, a ruler, graph paper, and some pencils. Simply measure your basement or attic floor space, then scale down the dimensions and transfer them to the graph paper. Add all obstacles, windows, doors, and other permanent fixtures. When everything is in place, start experimenting with different layouts. If you have your home's original blueprints, trace the floor plans onto tracing paper and work on new layouts from there.

Creating a successful layout takes time and often requires some creative problemsolving. To help generate ideas for your remodel, study the before-and-after drawings on page 101. While these floor plans may not look like your basement, they include many of the common elements and obstacles involved in a finishing project. They also show how carefully placed walls can transform an unfinished space into several livable areas that still leave room for storage and mechanical elements.

Basement Layouts: Before and After

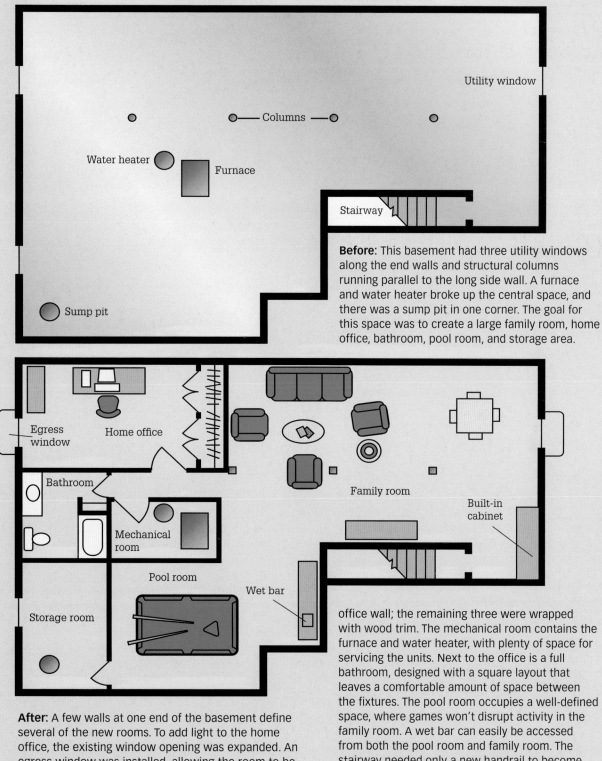

Utility window

Columns

Water heater

Furnace

Stairway

Sump pit

Before: This basement had three utility windows along the end walls and structural columns running parallel to the long side wall. A furnace and water heater broke up the central space, and there was a sump pit in one corner. The goal for this space was to create a large family room, home office, bathroom, pool room, and storage area.

Egress window

Home office

Bathroom

Mechanical room

Pool room

Storage room

Wet bar

Family room

Built-in cabinet

After: A few walls at one end of the basement define several of the new rooms. To add light to the home office, the existing window opening was expanded. An egress window was installed, allowing the room to be used as a bedroom as well. A larger window and well were installed to provide light and a better view from the family room. One column was hidden within the office wall; the remaining three were wrapped with wood trim. The mechanical room contains the furnace and water heater, with plenty of space for servicing the units. Next to the office is a full bathroom, designed with a square layout that leaves a comfortable amount of space between the fixtures. The pool room occupies a well-defined space, where games won't disrupt activity in the family room. A wet bar can easily be accessed from both the pool room and family room. The stairway needed only a new handrail to become code-compliant. At the bottom of the stairs, a built-in cabinet provides storage and adds a decorative touch to the basement entrance.

Shown cutaway for clarity

Wood laminate flooring

Dry-floor subfloor square

Underlayment

Basement slab

Most basement floors need some preparation before flooring can be laid. Patching compound and floor leveler can smooth rough concrete, while a subfloor system creates a new surface that is safe from moisture and feels like a framed wood floor.

Building Basement Floors

Preparing a concrete floor—for carpet, laminate, vinyl, or wood flooring—has changed for the better in dramatic fashion, thanks to new subfloor products that have built-in vapor barriers and cleats that create a slight air gap between the subfloor and the concrete slab. This system allows air to circulate, protecting the finished flooring from any slab moisture. The older method of laying ¾" plywood over a frame of 2 × 4 "sleepers" was difficult, time-consuming, and raised the floor level by 2" or more—a significant drawback in basements where ceiling levels may already be too low. The new dry-floor subfloor systems are less than 1" thick and are very easy to install. There are several types of these dry-floor systems available, but the one most readily available and easiest to use is a product sold in 2 × 2-ft. tongue-and-groove squares.

Although subfloor panels can be adjusted for slight irregularities in the concrete slab, they can't overcome problems with a floor that is badly cracked and heaved. Nor is the built-in air gap beneath the system a solution to a basement that has serious water problems. A badly heaved slab will need to be leveled with a cement-based leveling compound, and serious water problems will need to be rectified before you consider creating finished living space in a basement.

Allow the subfloor panel squares to acclimate in the basement for at least 24 hours with the plastic surfaces facing down before installing them. In humid summer months, the squares— as well as the finished wood flooring product, if that's what you'll be installing—should be allowed to acclimate for a full two weeks before installation.

To estimate the number of 2-ft.-square subfloor panels you'll need, calculate the size of the room in square feet (multiply the width times the length of the room), then divide by 3.3 to determine the number of panels required.

Tools & Materials Long straightedge ▪straightedge trowel ▪circular saw or jig saw ▪hammer ▪carpenter's square ▪flat pry bar ▪dust mask ▪ eye protection ▪Portland-cement–based leveling compound ▪dry-floor subfloor squares ▪leveling shims ▪flooring spacers.

Preparing Concrete Floors

Vacuum the floor thoroughly, then use a long straightedge to look for areas of the floor with serious dips or heaves. Note: Any old floor coverings that may trap moisture should be removed before installing subfloor panels.

Mix a batch of cement-based mortar and apply the compound to low areas with a straightedge trowel. After the patch dries, scrape the edges to feather the patch into the surrounding floor.

Installing Subfloor Panels

Beginning with the longest straight wall in the room, check one corner for square. If necessary, cut the first panel to match the angle of the corner. Position the panel in the corner, using ¼" spacers to create a gap between the panel and the walls, with the grooves of the panel against the spacers. Slide in the next panel, and use a piece of wood and a hammer to tap it firmly against the first panel. Repeat this placement along the entire wall. Cut the last panel to size.

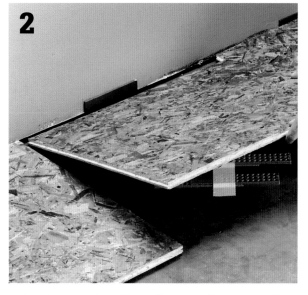

By hand, press along the entire row of panels, looking for low spots. At points where the subfloor flexes, lift the panels and place leveling shims on the floor. In some areas, you may find it necessary to stack two, three, or more shims to create the correct thickness to fill the low spot. Tape the shims to the floor to keep them in place as you reposition the panels.

(Continued next page)

Begin the next row of panels by cutting a half-wide panel, creating offset joints between the rows. Finish the second row, test it for flatness, and shim if necessary. Move on to the third row, this time beginning with a full panel. Work across the entire room in this fashion, testing each row for flatness, shimming where necessary, and making sure joints are offset between rows.

If the room has a floor drain, building code requires that you cut a round patch in the panel that falls directly over the floor drain. This patch can be removed to allow access to the floor drain should it ever be necessary.

For the last row of panels, measure and cut panels to fit, maintaining a ¼" gap between the panels and the wall. Work each panel into place with a flat pry bar. When all panels are in place, you can remove all spacers and continue with the installation of the finished flooring. Laminate flooring can be installed directly over the subfloor panels, but carpet, vinyl, or ceramic tile will require one of the variations on page 105.

Variation: Where slab moisture is known to be a problem, you can cut vent openings spaced every 8" to 12", sized to match standard metal floor vent covers. Trace the vent opening onto the panel, and cut the opening with a jig saw.

Variation: If carpeting will be stretched over the dry-floor panels, anchor the panels to the floor around the perimeter of the room and at the center of the room using concrete masonry anchors. Use a powder-actuated nailer to drive 2" nails through the panels and into the concrete slab.

Variation: For vinyl flooring or for engineered wood flooring, install ¼" plywood underlayment over the dry-floor panels, using ½" screws or nails, which won't penetrate the moisture barrier on the underside of the panels. (See page 103 for installing plywood.) Don't glue the plywood to the subfloor panels, and never glue vinyl flooring directly to the subfloor panels.

Variation: For ceramic tile, install ½" cementboard over the subfloor panels, and attach it using ¾" screws.

Where floor heights change, install transition strips or reducers, available in flooring departments of home improvement centers, to bridge the changes in floor heights.

Attic joists typically rest on top of exterior walls and on an interior load-bearing wall, where they overlap from side to side and are nailed together. Always use a sheet of plywood as a platform while working over open joists.

Building Attic Floors

Before you build the walls that will define the rooms in your attic, you'll need a sturdy floor beneath it all. Existing floors in most unfinished attics are merely ceiling joists for the floor below and are too small to support a living space.

There are several options for strengthening your attic's floor structure. The simplest method is to install an additional, identically sized joist next to each existing joist, connecting the two with nails. This process is known as *sistering*.

Sistering doesn't work when joists are smaller than 2 × 6s, are spaced too far apart, or where there are obstructions, such as plaster keys, from the ceiling below. An alternative is to build a new floor by placing larger joists between the existing ones. By resting the joists on 2 × 4 spacers, you avoid obstructions and minimize damage to the ceiling surface below. However, be aware that the spacers will reduce your headroom by 1½", plus the added joist depth.

To determine the best option for your attic, consult an architect, engineer, or building contractor, as well as a local building inspector. Ask what

size of joists you'll need and which options are allowed in your area. Joist sizing is based on the span (the distance between support points), the joist spacing (typically 16" or 24" on-center), and the type of lumber used. In most cases, an attic floor must be able to support 40 pounds per sq. ft. of *live load* (occupants, furniture) and 10 psf dead load (wallboard, floor covering).

The floor joist cavities offer space for concealing the plumbing, wiring, and ductwork servicing your attic, so consider these systems as you plan. You'll also need to locate partition walls to determine if any additional blocking between joists is necessary.

When the framing is done, the mechanical elements and insulation are in place, and everything has been inspected and approved, complete the floor by installing ¾" tongue-and-groove plywood. If your remodel will include kneewalls, you can omit the subflooring behind the kneewalls, but there are good reasons not to: A complete subfloor will add strength to the floor, and will provide a sturdy surface for storage.

Tools & Materials Circular saw ▪ rafter square ▪ drill ▪ caulk gun ▪ 2 × joist lumber ▪ 16d, 10d, and 8d common nails ▪ 2 × 4 lumber ▪ ¾" T&G plywood ▪ construction adhesive ▪ 2¼" wallboard screws.

How to Add Sister Joists

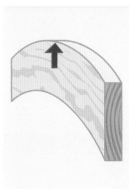

Before cutting, sight down both narrow edges of each board to check for crowning—upward arching along the length of the board. Draw an arrow that points in the direction of the arch. Joists must be installed "crown-up;" this arrow designates the top edge. Cut the board to length, then clip the top, outside corner to match the existing joists.

Remove all insulation from the joist cavities and carefully remove any blocking or bridging between the joists. Determine the lengths for the sister joists by measuring the existing joists. Also measure at the outside end of each joist to determine how much of the top corner was cut away to fit the joist beneath the roof sheathing. Note: Joists that rest on a bearing wall should overlap each other by at least 3".

Set the sister joists in place, flush against the existing joists and with their ends aligned. Toenail each sister joist to the top plates of both supporting walls, using two 16d common nails.

Nail the joists together using 10d common nails. Drive three nails in a row, spacing the rows 12" to 16" apart. To minimize damage to the ceiling surface below caused by the hammering (such as cracking and nail popping), you can use an air-powered nail gun (available at rental stores), or 3" lag screws instead of nails. Install new blocking between the sistered joists, as required by the local building code.

How to Build a New Attic Floor

Remove any blocking or bridging from between the existing joists, being careful not to disturb the ceiling below. Cut 2 × 4 spacers to fit snugly between each pair of joists. Lay the spacers flat against the top plate of all supporting walls, and nail them in place with 16d common nails.

Create a layout for the new joists by measuring across the tops of the existing joists and using a rafter square to transfer the measurements down to the spacers. Following 16"-on-center spacing, mark the layout along one exterior wall, then mark an identical layout onto the interior bearing wall. Note that the layout on the opposing exterior wall will be offset 1½", to account for the joist overlap at the interior wall.

To determine joist length, measure from the outer edge of the exterior wall to the far edge of the interior bearing wall. The joists must overlap each other above the interior wall by 3". Before cutting, mark the top edge of each joist. Cut the joists to length, then clip the top outside corners so the ends can fit under the roof sheathing.

Set the joists in place on their layout marks. Toenail the outside end of each joist to the spacer on the exterior wall, using three 8d common nails.

Nail the joists together where they overlap atop the interior bearing wall, using three 10d nails for each. Toenail the joists to the spacers on the interior bearing wall, using 8d nails.

Install blocking or bridging between the joists, as required by the local building code. As a suggested minimum, the new joists should be blocked as close as possible to the outside ends and where they overlap at the interior wall.

How to Install Subflooring

Subflooring

Joist

2 × 4 Backing

Install the subflooring only after all framing, plumbing, wiring, and ductwork is completed and has received the required building inspections. Also install any insulation and complete any caulking necessary for soundproofing. Fasten the sheets with construction adhesive and 2¼" wallboard or deck screws, making sure the sheets are perpendicular to the joists and the end joints are staggered between rows. Where joists overlap at an interior bearing wall, add backing as needed to compensate for the offset in the layout. Nail a 2 × 4 or wider board to the face of each joist to support the edges of the intervening sheets.

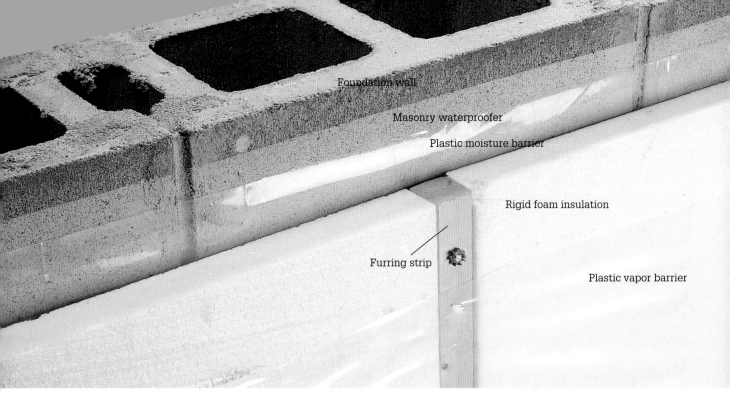

Foundation wall

Masonry waterproofer

Plastic moisture barrier

Rigid foam insulation

Furring strip

Plastic vapor barrier

Local building codes may require a barrier to prevent moisture from damaging wood and insulation covering foundation walls. This may be masonry waterproofer, or plastic sheeting placed behind or in front of the framing.

Covering Basement Walls

There are two common methods for covering foundation walls. Because it saves space, the more popular method is to attach 2 × 2 furring strips directly to the masonry wall. These strips provide a 1½"-deep cavity between strips for insulation and service lines, as well as a framework for attaching wallboard. The other method is to build a complete 2 × 4 stud wall just in front of the foundation wall. This method offers a full 3½" for insulation and lines, and it provides a flat, plumb wall surface, regardless of the foundation wall's condition.

To determine the best method for your project, examine the foundation walls. If they're fairly plumb and flat, you can consider furring them. If the walls are wavy or out of plumb, however, it may be easier to build stud walls. Also check with the local building department before you decide on a framing method.

There may be codes regarding insulation minimums and methods of running service lines along foundation walls.

A local building official can also tell you what's recommended—or required—in your area for sealing foundation walls against moisture. Common types of moisture barriers include masonry waterproofers that are applied like paint and plastic sheeting installed between masonry walls and wood framing. The local building code will also specify whether you need a vapor barrier between the framing and the wallboard.

Before you shop for materials, decide how you'll fasten the wood framing to your foundation walls and floor. If you're covering a large wall area, it will be worth it to buy or rent a powder-actuated nailer for the job.

Tools & Materials
Caulk gun ▪ trowel ▪ paint rolle ▪ circular saw ▪ drill ▪ powder-actuated nailer ▪ plumb bob ▪ Paper-faced insulation ▪ silicone caulk ▪ hydraulic cement ▪ masonry waterproofer ▪ 2 × 2 and 2 × 4 lumber ▪ 2½" wallboard screws ▪ construction adhesive ▪ concrete fasteners ▪ insulation.

How to Seal and Prepare Masonry Walls

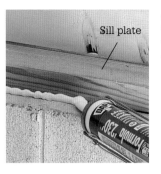

Apply silicone caulk to the joints between the sill plates and the foundation walls.

Insulate the rim-joist cavities (above the foundation walls) with solid pieces of paper-faced fiberglass insulation. Make sure the paper, which serves as a vapor barrier, faces the room.

Fill small cracks with hydraulic cement or masonry caulk, and smooth the excess with a trowel. Ask the building department whether masonry waterproofer or a plastic moisture barrier is required in your area. Apply waterproofer as directed by the manufacturer, or install plastic sheeting following code specifications.

Options for Attaching Wood to Masonry

Masonry nails are the cheapest way to attach wood to concrete block walls. Drive the nails into the mortar joints for maximum holding power and to avoid cracking the blocks. Drill pilot holes through the strips if the nails cause splitting. Masonry nails are difficult to drive into poured concrete.

Self-tapping masonry screws hold well in block or poured concrete, but they must be driven into predrilled holes. Use a hammer drill to drill holes of the same size in both the wood and the concrete after the wood is positioned. Drive the screws into the web portion of the blocks.

Powder-actuated nailers offer the quickest and easiest method for fastening framing to block, poured concrete, and steel. They use individual caps of gunpowder—called loads—to propel a piston that drives a hardened-steel nail (pin) through the wood and into the masonry. The loads are color-coded for the charge they produce, and the pins come in various lengths. Note: Always drive pins into the solid web portions of concrete blocks, not into the voids. Trigger-type nailers, like the one shown here, are easiest to use, but hammer-activated types are also available. You can buy nailers at home centers and hardware stores, or rent them from rental centers. (Ask for a demonstration at the rental center.) Always wear hearing and eye protection when using these extremely loud tools.

How to Install Furring Strips on Masonry Walls

Cut a 2 × 2 top plate to span the length of the wall. Mark the furring-strip layout onto the bottom edge of the plate, using 16"-on-center spacing. Attach the plate to the bottom of the joists with 2½" wallboard screws. The back edge of the plate should line up with the front of the blocks.

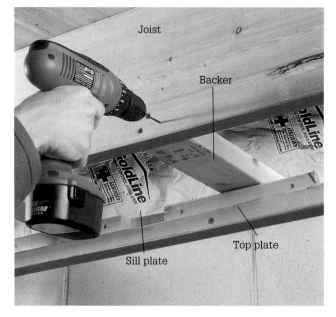

Note: If the joists run parallel to the wall, you'll need to install backers between the outer joist and the sill plate to provide support for ceiling wallboard. Make T-shaped backers from short 2 × 4s and 2 × 2s. Install each so the bottom face of the 2 × 4 is flush with the bottom edge of the joists. Attach the top plate to the foundation wall with its top edge flush with the top of the blocks.

Install a bottom plate cut from pressure-treated 2 × 2 lumber so the plate spans the length of the wall. Apply construction adhesive to the back and bottom of the plate, then attach it to the floor with a nailer. Use a plumb bob to transfer the furring-strip layout marks from the top plate to the bottom plate.

Cut 2 × 2 furring strips to fit between the top and bottom plates. Apply construction adhesive to the back of each furring strip, and position it on the layout marks on the plates. Nail along the length of each strip at 16" intervals.

Option: Leave a channel for the installation of wires or supply pipes by installing pairs of vertically aligned furring strips with a 2" gap between each pair. Note: Consult local codes to ensure proper installation of electrical or plumbing materials.

Fill the cavities between furring strips with rigid insulation board. Cut the pieces so they fit snugly within the framing. If necessary, make cutouts in the insulation to fit around mechanical elements, and cover any channels with metal protective plates before attaching the wall surface. Add a vapor barrier if required by local building code.

Tips for Covering Foundation Walls with Stud Walls

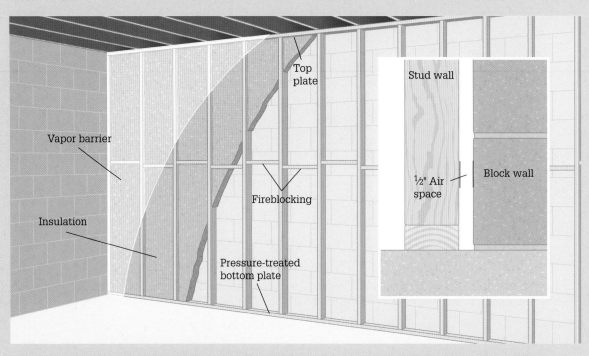

Build a standard 2 × 4 partition wall. Use pressure-treated lumber for any bottom plates that rest on concrete. To minimize moisture problems and avoid unevenness in foundation walls, leave a ½" air space between the stud walls and the masonry walls (inset). Insulate the stud walls with fiberglass blankets, and install a vapor barrier if required by local code. Also install all fireblocking required by local code.

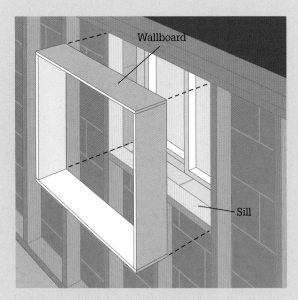

Frame around a basement window so the framing is flush with the edges of the masonry on all sides. Install a sill at the base of the window opening, and add a header, if necessary. Fill the space between the framing members and the masonry with fiberglass insulation or non-expanding foam insulation. Install wallboard so it butts against the window frame.

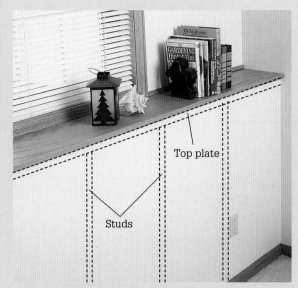

Build a short stud wall to cover a low foundation wall in a walkout or "daylight" basement. Install the top plate flush with the top of the foundation wall. Finish the wall surface with wallboard or other finish, then cap the walls with finish-grade lumber or plywood to create a decorative shelf.

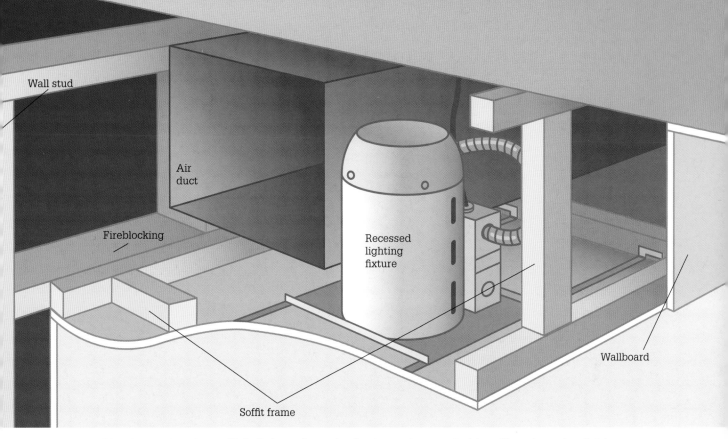

Wall stud

Air duct

Fireblocking

Recessed lighting fixture

Wallboard

Soffit frame

Hide immovable obstructions in a soffit built from dimension lumber and covered with wallboard or other finish material. An extra-wide soffit is also a great place to install recessed lighting fixtures.

Framing Soffits & Chases

Your unfinished basement or attic is sure to have beams, pipes, posts, ductwork, and other elements that are vital to your house but become big obstacles to finishing the space. When you can't conceal the obstructions within walls, and you've determined it's too costly to move them, hide them inside a framed soffit or chase. This can also provide a place to run smaller mechanicals, like wiring and water supply lines.

Soffits and chases are easy to build. A soffit is usually constructed with 2 × 2 lumber, which is easy to work with and inexpensive. You can use 1 × 3s to keep the frame as small as possible and 2 × 4s for large soffits that will house other elements, such as lighting fixtures. Chases should be framed with 2 × 4s.

This section shows you some basic techniques for building soffits and chases, but the design of your framing is up to you. For example, you may want to shape your soffits for a decorative effect, or build an oversized chase that holds bookshelves. Just make sure the framing conforms to local building codes. There may be code restrictions about the types of mechanicals that can be grouped together, as well as minimum clearances between the framing and what it encloses. And most codes specify that soffits, chases, and other framed structures have fireblocking every 10 ft. and at the intersections between soffits and neighboring walls. Remember, too, that drain cleanouts and shutoff valves must be accessible, so you'll need to install access panels at these locations.

Tools & Materials Circular saw ▪ drill ▪ powder-actuated nailer ▪ Standard lumber (1 × 3, 2 × 2, 2 × 4) ▪ pressure-treated 2 × 4s ▪ construction adhesive ▪ wallboard ▪ unfaced fiberglass insulation ▪ nails ▪ wood trim ▪ plywood ▪ wallboard screws ▪ decorative screws.

Variations for Building Soffits

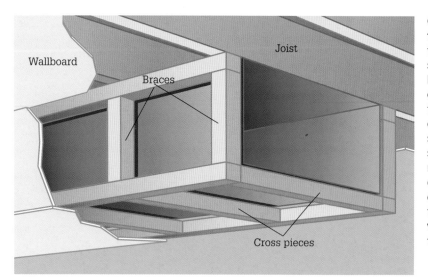

Obstructions perpendicular to joists. Build two ladder-like frames for the soffit sides, using standard 2 × 2s. Install 2 × 2 braces (or "rungs") every 16" or 24" to provide nailing support for the edges of the wallboard or other finish material. Attach the side frames to the joists on either side of the obstruction, using nails or screws. Then, install cross pieces beneath the obstacle, tying the two sides together. Cover the soffit with wallboard, plywood, or other finish material.

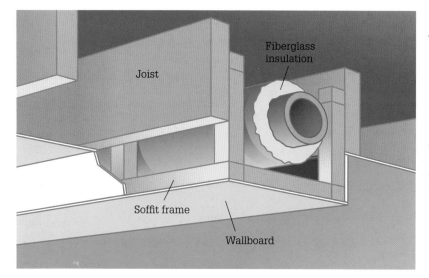

Obstructions parallel to joists. Build side frames as with perpendicular obstructions, but size them to fit in between two joists. This provides nailing surfaces for both the soffit and ceiling finish materials. Attach the frames to the joists with screws, then install cross pieces. Note: If you are enclosing a drain pipe, wrap the pipe in unfaced fiberglass insulation to muffle the sound of draining water.

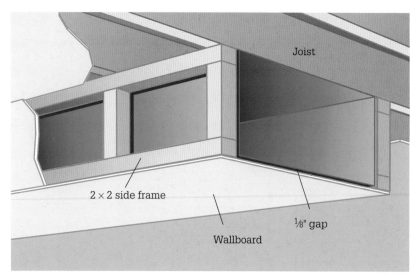

Maximize headroom. In rooms with low ceilings, and where an obstruction is less than 12" wide and the finish material will be wallboard or plywood, build side frames (see above) so that the bottom edges are 1/8" lower than the lowest point of the obstruction. For soffits of this width, the bottom piece of wallboard or plywood stabilizes the structure, so cross pieces between side frames aren't necessary.

How To Frame a Chase

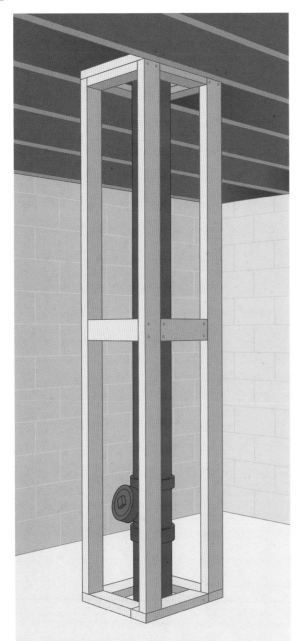

Build chases with 2 × 4s, which tend to be straighter than 2 × 2s and are strong enough to withstand household accidents. Use pressure-treated lumber for bottom plates on concrete floors, attaching them with construction adhesive and powder-actuated nailer fasteners. Cut top plates from standard lumber and nail or screw them in place. Install studs to form the corners of the chase, and block in between them for stability. To make the chase smaller, notch the top and bottom plates around the obstruction, and install the studs flat. If you're framing around a vertical drain pipe (especially the main DWV stack), leave room around the pipe for soundproofing insulation; plastic pipes can be especially noisy.

How to Make Access Panels

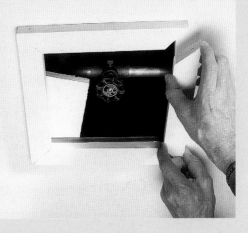

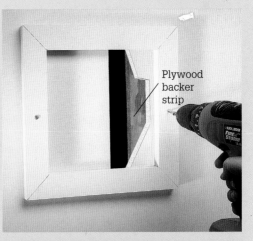

Plywood backer strip

After your soffits and chases are framed, note the locations of all access points before you install the wallboard. Make the access panels after the wallboard is installed.

In a horizontal surface (top photo), cut out a square piece of wallboard at the access location. Push the cutout through the opening and slide it to one side so it rests on the inside of the soffit. Glue mitered trim around the opening so it overlaps the opening by approximately ½" on all sides. Position the panel so it rests on the trim and can be moved when necessary.

In a vertical surface (bottom photo), cut an opening in the same fashion, and glue mitered trim to the edges of the cutout to create the panel. Install plywood backer strips to the back of the wallboard at two sides of the opening. Position the finished panel over the opening so it rests against the strips. Drill pilot holes through the trim, and secure the panel to the backer strips with decorative screws.

Building Partition Walls

Non-loadbearing, or partition walls are typically built with 2 × 4 lumber and are supported by ceiling or floor joists above or by blocking between the joists. For basement walls that sit on bare concrete, use pressure-treated lumber for the bottom plates.

This project shows you how to build a wall in place, rather than how to build a complete wall on the floor and tilt it upright, as in new construction. The build-in-place method allows for variations in floor and ceiling levels and is generally much easier for remodeling projects.

If your wall will include a door or other opening, see page 126 before laying out the wall. Note: After your walls are framed and the mechanical rough-ins are completed, be sure to install metal protector plates where pipes and wires run through framing members.

Tools & Materials
Chalk line ■ circular saw ■ framing square ■ plumb bob ■ powder-actuated nailer ■ T-bevel ■ 2 × 4 lumber ■ blocking lumber ■ 16d and 8d common nails ■ concrete fasteners ■ wallboard screws

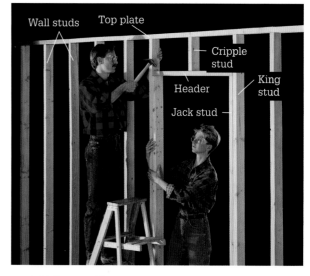

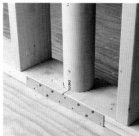

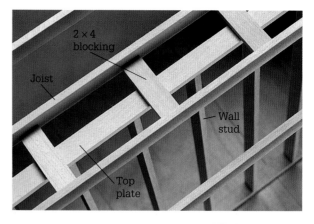

A typical partition wall consists of top and bottom plates and 2 × 4 studs spaced 16" on center. Use 2 × 6 lumber for walls that will hold large plumbing pipes (inset).

Variations for Fastening Top Plates to Joists

When a new wall is perpendicular to the ceiling or floor joists above, attach the top plate directly to the joists, using 16d nails.

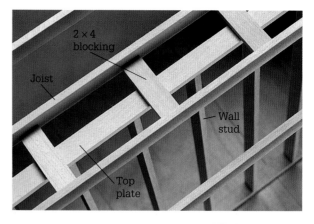

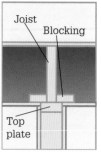

When a new wall falls between parallel joists, install 2 × 4 blocking between the joists every 24". The blocking supports the new wall's top plate and provides backing for the ceiling wallboard. If the new wall is aligned with a parallel joist, install blocks on both sides of the wall, and attach the top plate to the joist.

Variations for Fastening Bottom Plates to Joists

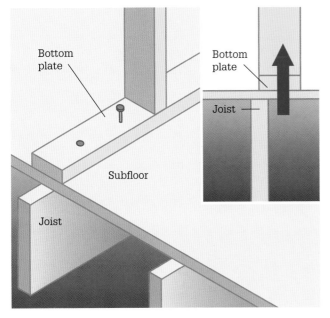

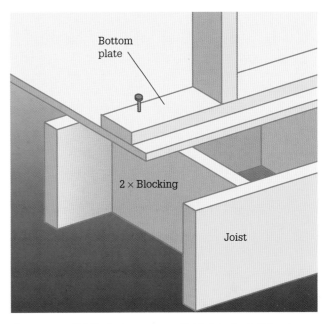

If a new wall is aligned with a joist below, install the bottom plate directly over the joist or off-center over the joist (inset). Off-center placement allows you to nail into the joist but provides room underneath the plate for pipes or wiring to go up into the wall.

If a new wall falls between parallel joists, install 2 × 6 or larger blocking between the two joists below, spaced 24" on center. Nail the bottom plate through the subfloor and into the blocking.

How to Build a Partition Wall

Mark the location of the leading edge of the new wall's top plate, then snap a chalk line through the marks across the joists or blocks. Use a framing square, or take measurements, to make sure the line is perpendicular to any intersecting walls. Cut the top and bottom plates to length.

Set the plates together with their ends flush. Measure from the end of one plate, and make marks for the location of each stud. The first stud should fall 15¼" from the end; every stud thereafter should fall 16" on center. Thus, the first 4 × 8-ft. wallboard panel will cover the first stud and "break" in the center of the fourth stud. Use a square to extend the marks across both plates. Draw an "X" at each stud location.

(Continued next page)

3

Position the top plate against the joists, aligning its leading edge with the chalk line. Attach the plate with two 16d nails driven into each joist. Start at one end and adjust the plate as you go to keep the leading edge flush with the chalk line.

4

To position the bottom plate, hang a plumb bob from the side edge of the top plate so the point nearly touches the floor. When it hangs motionless, mark the point's location on the floor. Make plumb markings at each end of the top plate, then snap a chalk line between the marks. Position the bottom plate along the chalk line, and use the plumb bob to align the stud markings between the two plates.

5

Fasten the bottom plate to the floor. On concrete, use a powder-actuated nailer or masonry screws driving a pin or screw every 16". On wood floors, use 16d nails driven into the joists or sleepers below.

6

Measure between the plates for the length of each stud. Cut each stud so it fits snugly in place but is not so tight that it bows the joists above. If you cut a stud too short, see if it will fit somewhere else down the wall.

7

Install the studs by toenailing them at a 60° angle through the sides of the studs and into the plates. At each end, drive two 8d nails through one side of the stud and one more through the center on the other side.

How to Frame Corners

1

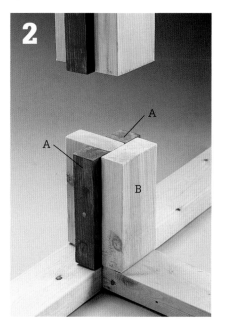

2

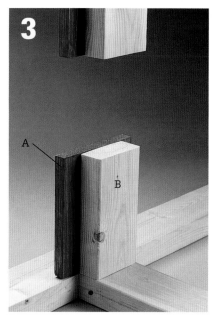

3

L-corners: Nail 2 × 4 spacers (A) to the inside of the end stud. Nail an extra stud (B) to the spacers. The extra stud provides a surface to attach wallboard at the inside corner.

T-corner meets stud: Fasten 2 × 2 backers (A) to each side of the side-wall stud (B). The backers provide a nailing surface for wallboard.

T-corner between studs: Fasten a 1 × 6 backer (A) to the end stud (B) with wallboard screws. The backer provides a nailing surface for wallboard.

How to Frame an Angled Partition Wall in an Attic

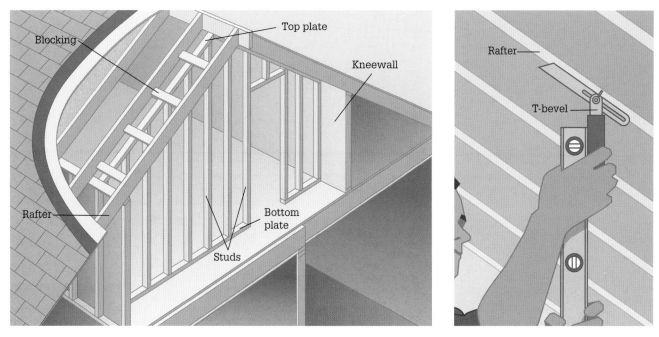

Full-size attic partition walls typically run parallel to the rafters and have sloping top plates that extend down to kneewalls on either side. To build one, cut the top and bottom plates, and mark the stud locations on the bottom plate only. Nail the top plates in place, and use a plumb bob to position the bottom plate, as with a standard wall. Use the plumb bob again to transfer the stud layout marks from the bottom to the top plate. To find the proper angle for cutting the top ends of the studs, set a level against the top plate (or rafter) and hold it plumb. Then, rest the handle of a T-bevel against the level, and adjust the T-bevel blade to follow the plate. Transfer the angle to the stud ends, and cut them to length.

Building Attic Kneewalls

Attic kneewalls are short walls that extend from the attic floor to the rafters. They provide a vertical dimension to attic rooms, and without them, attics tend to feel cramped. Kneewalls are typically 5 ft. tall, for a couple of reasons: That's the minimum ceiling height for usable floor space according to most building codes, and it defines a comfortable room without wasting too much floor space. The unfinished space behind kneewalls doesn't have to go to waste: It's great for storage and for concealing service lines. To provide access to this space, create a framed opening in the wall during the framing process.

Kneewalls are similar to partition walls, except they have beveled top plates and angle-cut studs that follow the slope of the rafters. The added stud depth created by the angled cut requires a 2 × 6 top plate. Before starting on your kneewall project, it may help to review the techniques for building a partition wall (see page 118).

Tools & Materials   Circular saw ▪ level ▪ chalk line
▪ T-bevel ▪ 2 × 4 and 2 × 6 lumber ▪ 16d ▪ 8d common nails.

Attic kneewalls are just the right height to be backdrops for furniture, and they make a perfect foundation for built-in storage units.

How to Build a Kneewall

Create a storyboard using a straight 2 × 4. Cut the board a few inches longer than the planned height of the wall. Measure from one end and draw a line across the front edge of the board at the exact wall height.

At one end of the room, set the storyboard flat against the outer rafter. Plumb the storyboard with a level while aligning the height mark with the bottom edge of the rafter. Transfer the height mark onto the rafter edge, then make a mark along the front edge of the storyboard onto the subfloor. These marks represent the top and bottom wall plates.

3

Holding the storyboard perfectly plumb, trace along the bottom edge of the rafter to transfer the rafter slope onto the face of the storyboard.

4

Repeat the wall-plate marking process on the other end of the room. Snap a chalk line through the marks—across the rafters and along the subfloor. If necessary, add backing for fastening the top plate to the gable wall.

To cut a beveled edge on the top wall plate, set a T-bevel to match the rafter-slope line on the storyboard. Use the T-bevel to adjust the blade of a circular saw or table saw to the proper angle. Then, bevel-cut one edge of the 2 × 6 top plate. Note: When the top plate is laid flat across the rafters, the front edge should be perpendicular to the floor.

5

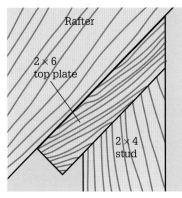

Rafter

2 × 6 top plate

2 × 4 stud

6

Mark the stud locations on the wall plates. Install the plates along the chalk lines, fastening them to the rafters and floor joists, respectively, using 16d nails. Measure and cut each stud to fit, angle-cutting the top end so that it meets flush with the top plate. Toenail each stud in place with three 8d nails.

Flat attic ceilings provide space for recessed light fixtures, vents, and speakers.

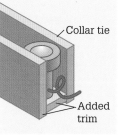

Exposed collar ties can add an interesting architectural element to a peaked ceiling. By adding to the existing ties, you can create a channel for holding small light fixtures.

Collar tie

Added trim

Framing Attic Ceilings

By virtue of sloping roofs, most attics naturally have "cathedral" ceilings. It's up to you whether to leave the peaks intact—and apply a finish surface all the way up to the ridge—or to frame-in a horizontal ceiling, creating a flat surface that's more like a standard ceiling. Before deciding, consider the advantages and disadvantages of each treatment.

If your attic has collar ties—horizontal braces installed between opposing rafters—your planning should start with those. Are the ties high enough to meet the code requirements for attic headroom? If not, consult an architect or engineer to see if you can move them up a few inches (do not move or remove them without professional guidance). If the ties are high enough, you can incorporate them into a new ceiling or leave them exposed and wrap them with a finish material, such as wallboard or finish-grade lumber. Do not use collar ties as part of your ceiling frame.

A peaked ceiling is primarily an aesthetic option. Its height expands the visual space of the room, and its rising angles provide a dramatic look that's unique in most homes. Because a peaked ceiling encloses the rafter bays all the way up to the ridge, this treatment may require additional roof vents to maintain proper ventilation.

By contrast, a flat ceiling typically offers a cleaner, more finished appearance closer to that of a conventional room, and flat ceilings offer some practical advantages over peaked styles. First, they provide a concealed space above the ceiling, great for running service lines. If there are vents high on the gable walls, this open space can help ventilate the roof (make sure to insulate above the ceiling). The ceiling itself can hold recessed lighting fixtures or support a ceiling fan. And if your plans call for full-height partition walls, you may want a ceiling frame to enclose the top of the wall.

When determining the height of flat-ceiling framing, be sure to account for the floor and ceiling finishes. And remember that most building codes require a finished ceiling height of at least 90".

Tools & Materials 4-ft. level ▪ chalk line ▪ circular saw ▪ 2 × 4 and 2 × 6 lumber ▪ 10d common nails

How to Frame a Flat Ceiling

Make a storyboard for the planned height of the ceiling frame. At one end of the attic, hold the storyboard plumb and align the height mark with the bottom edge of a rafter. Transfer the mark to the rafter. Repeat at the other end of the attic, then snap a chalk line through the marks. This line represents the bottom edge of the ceiling frame.

Using a level and the storyboard, level over from the chalk line and mark two outside rafters on the other side of the attic. Snap a chalk line through the marks. Note: The storyboard is used merely as a straightedge for this step.

Cut 2 × 6 joists to span across the rafters, angle-cutting the ends to follow the roof pitch. Check each joist for crowning to make sure you're cutting it so it will be installed with the crowned edge up. Make the overall length about ½" short so the ends of the joists won't touch the roof sheathing.

Nail each joist to the rafters with three 10d common nails at each end. Be sure to maintain 16"- or 24"- on-center spacing between joists to provide support for attaching wallboard or other finish material.

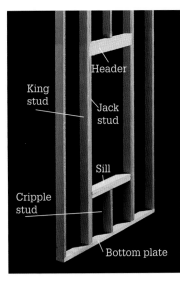

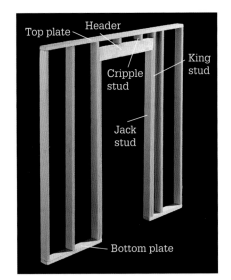

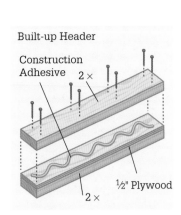

Window frames, like door frames, have full-length king studs, as well as jack studs that support the header. They also have a *sill* that defines the bottom of the rough opening.

Door frames for prehung doors start with *king* studs that attach to the top and bottom plates. Inside the king studs, *jack* studs support the *header* at the top of the opening. *Cripple* studs continue the wall-stud layout above the opening. In non-load-bearing walls, the header may be a 2 × 4 laid flat or a built-up header. The dimensions of the framed opening are referred to as the rough opening.

Framing Doors & Windows

In new walls, build your door frames along with the rest of the wall. The project shown here demonstrates framing a rough opening for an interior prehung door in a new, non-load-bearing partition wall. The basic steps are the same for closet doors. However, for large closet openings, such as for double bi-fold or by-pass doors, use a built-up header: two 2 × 4s set on edge and nailed together with a strip of ½"-thick plywood in between. This provides additional strength to support the weight of the doors.

Although most windows in a house are located in load-bearing exterior walls, standard attic windows are commonly located in gable walls, which often are non-load-bearing. Installing a window in a non-load-bearing gable wall is fairly simple and doesn't require temporary support for the framing. Some gable walls, however, are load-bearing: A common sign is a heavy structural ridge beam that supports the rafters from underneath, rather than merely at the rafter ends. Hire a contractor to build

window frames in load-bearing gable walls. If you aren't certain what type of wall you have, consult a professional.

A common problem with framing in a gable wall is that the positions of the floor joists may make it difficult to attach new studs to the bottom wall plate. One solution is to install an extra-long header and sill between two existing studs, positioning them at the precise heights for the rough opening. You can then adjust the width of the rough opening by installing vertical studs between the header and sill.

When planning the placement of attic windows, remember that the bottom of an egress window must be no higher than 44" from the finished floor. Windows lower than 24" may require tempered glazing.

To lay out and build a door or window frame, you'll need the actual dimensions of the door or window unit, so it's best to have the unit on hand for the framing process.

Tools & Materials   Circular saw ▪ handsaw ▪ plumb
bob ▪ T-bevel ▪ 4-ft. level, combination square ▪ reciprocating saw
▪ Framed door or window unit; 2 × 4 lumber ▪ 16d, 10d, and 8d
common nails ▪ ½"-thick plywood ▪ construction adhesive

How to Frame a Rough Opening for an Interior Prehung Door

King stud marking

Door unit width

Extra ½"

Extra ½"

King stud marking

Jack stud marking

Jack stud marking

To mark the layout for the studs that make up the door frame, measure the width of the door unit along the bottom. Add 1" to this dimension to calculate the width of the rough opening (the distance between the jack studs). This gives you a ½" gap on each side for adjusting the door frame during installation. Mark the top and bottom plates for the jack and king studs.

After you've installed the wall plates, cut the king studs and toenail them in place at the appropriate markings.

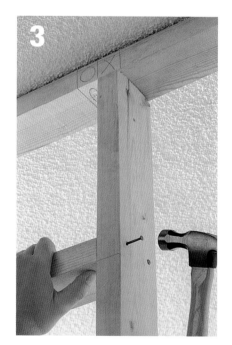

Measure the full length of the door unit, then add ½" to determine the height of the rough opening. Using that dimension, measure up from the floor and mark the king studs. Cut a 2 × 4 header to fit between the king studs. Position the header flat, with its bottom face at the marks, and secure it to the king studs with 16d nails.

Cut and install a cripple stud above the header, centered between the king studs. Install any additional cripples required to maintain the 16"-on-center layout of the standard studs in the rest of the wall.

(Continued next page)

5

Cut the jack studs to fit snugly under the header. Fasten them in place by nailing down through the header, then drive 10d nails through the faces of the jack studs and into the king studs, spaced 16" apart.

6

Saw through the bottom plate so it's flush with the inside faces of the jack studs. Remove the cut-out portion of the plate. Note: If the wall will be finished with wallboard, hang the door after the wallboard is installed.

How to Frame a Window Opening in a Gable Wall (non-loadbearing)

1

Determine the rough opening width by measuring the window unit and adding 1". Add 3" to that dimension to get the distance between the king studs. Mark the locations of the king studs onto the bottom plate of the gable wall.

2

Using a plumb bob, transfer the king stud marks from the bottom plate to the sloping top plates of the gable wall.

3

Cut the king studs to length, angle-cutting the top ends so they meet flush with the top plates. Fasten each king stud in place by toenailing the ends with three 8d nails.

Find the height of the rough opening by measuring the height of the window unit and adding ½". Measure up from where the finished floor height will be, and mark the top of the sill. Make a second mark for the bottom of the sill, 3" down from the top mark.

Measure up from the top sill mark, and mark the height of the rough opening (bottom of header). Make another mark 3½" up, to indicate the top of the header. Using a level, transfer all of these marks to the other king stud and to all intermediate studs.

Draw level cutting lines across the intermediate studs at the marks for the bottom of the sill and top of the header. Cut along the lines with a reciprocating saw, then remove the cut-out portions. The remaining stud sections will serve as cripple studs.

Cut the jack studs to reach from the bottom plate to the bottom header marks on the king studs. Nail the jack studs to the inside faces of the king studs using 10d common nails driven every 16".

Build a built-up header with 2 × 4s and plywood (see page 126). Size the header to fit snugly between the king studs. Set the header on top of the jack studs. Nail through the king studs into the header with 16d nails, then toenail the jack studs and cripple studs to the header, using 8d nails.

Build the sill to fit snugly between the jack studs by nailing together two 2 × 4s. Position the sill at the top sill markings, and toenail it to the jack studs. Toenail the cripple studs to the sill.

Basement window openings must have support above to carry the weight of the house. An opening in masonry is usually fitted with wood bucks to serve as a rough window frame.

Egress windows in basements require large wells that meet code specifications. The prefabricated window well shown here has a stepped side that serves as stairs for emergency escape. Spaces behind the steps can hold plants to dress up the view from the window.

Enlarging Basement Window Openings

Whether the goal is to add more natural light or to provide emergency egress, enlarging a window opening for a new window is a common project for basement remodels. However, it's not always a do-it-yourself job. There are many factors to consider, and depending on your basement configuration and the size of window you want, it may be best to hire a professional to do some or all of the work. If you want to add a window where none already exists, have a professional create the new opening for you.

The first, and most important, consideration is ensuring there will be adequate support for your house once the window opening is expanded or created. If you're not changing the width of the opening, the means for support should already be in place. Increasing the opening's width, however, will require a new wood header or a steel lintel to span the top of the opening and carry the weight from above.

The second consideration is the window well, which must be dug before the window can be expanded. Digging a window well can be a fairly extensive project; the discussion of window wells on page 133 gives you an idea of what's involved.

After preparing the well comes the task of cutting into the foundation wall. With concrete block, this is a messy job but surprisingly easy. If your foundation walls are poured concrete, you'll need to have a professional cut the opening. For many window types, the rough opening in the masonry must be wrapped with dimension lumber to provide a frame for fastening the window. The lumber pieces—called *bucks*—are usually 2 × 10s or 2 × 12s and should cover the width of the block. To prevent rotting from moisture, use pressure-treated lumber for the window bucks.

Tools & Materials Level ▪ masonry chisel ▪ hand maul ▪ circular saw ▪ masonry saw blade ▪ masonry hammer ▪ trowel ▪ drill ▪ hammer drill ▪ masonry bit ▪ caulk gun ▪ Concrete ▪ construction adhesive ▪ pressure-treated 2 × lumber ▪ self-tapping masonry screws ▪ silicone caulk

How to Enlarge a Window Opening in a Concrete Wall Block

Remove the old window unit and frame, then mark the rough opening on both the interior and exterior surfaces of the wall, using a level as a guide.

Score the cutting lines, using a masonry chisel and hand maul. Be sure to wear eye protection and work gloves.

Cut along the scored lines with a circular saw and masonry blade. Make several passes with the saw, gradually deepening the cut until the saw blade is at maximum depth.

Break both the inside and outside mortar lines on all sides of the center block in the top row of the area being removed.

(Continued next page)

Strike the face of the center block with a masonry hammer until the block either comes loose or breaks into pieces.

Chip out large pieces, then break the mortar around the remaining blocks. Chip out the remaining blocks using the chisel and maul.

Create a smooth surface by filling the hollow areas in the cut blocks with broken pieces of concrete block, then troweling in fresh concrete. Make sure all of the surfaces are flat. Let the concrete dry overnight.

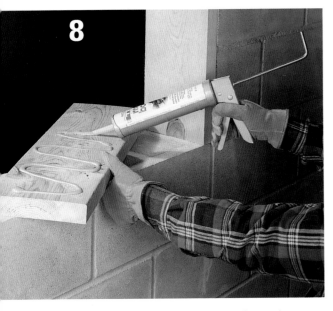

Cut pressure-treated 2 × lumber to frame the opening. If necessary, rip-cut the bucks to width so they are flush with the block on both sides. Apply construction adhesive to the bucks and set them in place.

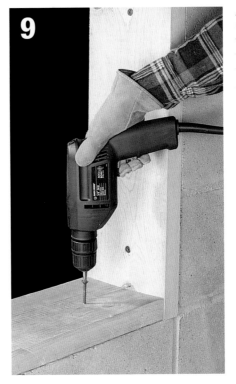

Anchor the bucks by drilling pilot holes with a masonry bit, then driving self-tapping masonry screws into the blocks, spaced every 10". Seal the joints between the bucks and the masonry with silicone caulk—on both sides of the wall.

Planning for Window Wells

Window wells for standard basement windows are usually small steel shells that let in very little natural light. If your basement project includes expanding existing window openings or adding new ones, you'll need wells that make the most of the new windows. If you're adding an egress window for a bedroom or as a secondary fire escape, the window well must be built to strict building code specifications. There are also some general considerations for wells, such as appearance, size, and drainage.

Window wells can be made of a variety of different materials. Prefabricated wells include the standard corrugated steel type that you can buy at home centers and specialty units made of polyethylene. For a custom-built well, you can use concrete block, landscaping timbers, and boulders.

Sizing for a window well depends on several factors. First, the well must extend far enough from the foundation to accommodate the window's operation. For example, casement windows need more room than sliders. Secondly, the size of the well affects how much light reaches the window. While a bigger well lets in more light than a smaller one, it also creates a larger hole that children or pets can fall into if it is uncovered, and a large well collects more water. As general minimums, a window well should be about 6" wider than the window opening, and should extend at least 18" from the foundation wall. And all wells should extend 8" below the window sill and 4" above grade.

The minimum dimensions for an egress-window well will be determined by your local building code. Typically, wells for egress windows must be at least 9 sq. ft. overall, measure at least 36" in width, and extend 36" from the foundation wall. Wells more than 44" deep must have a permanently attached ladder or a step system that doesn't interfere with the window's operation.

Providing adequate drainage for your window wells is particularly important if you plan to leave them uncovered. All wells should have a layer of gravel that is at least 6" deep and stops 3" below the window frame. Uncovered wells, however, may need a drain pipe or a continuous layer of gravel that leads to the footing drain or other perimeter drain system.

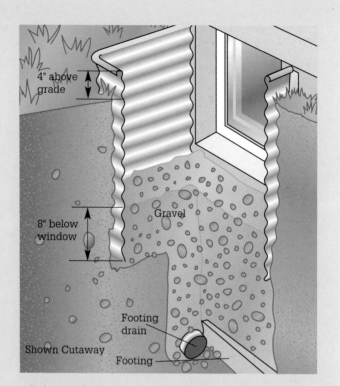

Window wells should extend 8" below the window frame and 4" above the ground. Wells for egress windows must be at least 36" wide and project 36" from the foundation, and those deeper than 44" must have a ladder or other means of escape. To keep water from pooling near the window, well bases should have a 6" layer of gravel. More extensive drainage can be provided by gravel that passes water down to a footing drain or by a well drain leading to daylight.

Plastic well covers keep rain, snow, and debris from entering your well. Covers on egress-window wells must be hinged or easily removable from inside the well.

Because they are set into thick foundation walls, basement windows present a bit of a trimming challenge. But the thickness of the foundation wall also lets you create a handy ledge that's deep enough to hold potted plants or even sunning cats.

Trimming Basement Windows

Basement windows bring much-needed sunlight into dark areas, but even in finished basements they often get ignored on the trim front. This is partly because most basement foundation walls are at least 8" thick, and often a lot thicker. Add a furred-out wall and the window starts to look more like a tunnel with a pane of glass at the end. But with some well designed and well-executed trim carpentry, you can turn the depth disadvantage into a positive.

A basement window opening may be finished with wallboard, but the easiest way to trim one is by making extra–wide custom jambs that extend from the inside face of the window frame to the interior wall surface. Because of the extra width, plywood stock is a good choice for the custom jambs. The project shown here is created with veneer-core plywood with oak veneer surface. The jamb members are fastened together into a nice square frame using rabbet joints at the corner. The frame is scribed and installed as a single unit and then trimmed out with oak casing. The casing is applied flush with the inside edges of the frame opening. If you prefer to have a reveal edge around the interior edge of the casing, you will need to add a solid hardwood strip to the edge of the frame so the plies of the plywood are not visible.

Tools & Materials pencil ▪ tape measure, table saw ▪ drill with bits ▪ 2-ft level ▪ framing square ▪ utility knife ▪ straightedge ▪ finish-grade ¾" oak plywood ▪ spray-foam insulation ▪ composite or cedar wood shims ▪ 1¼, 2" finish nails ▪ 1⅝" drywall screws ▪ carpenter's glue

How to Trim a Basement Window

Check to make sure the window frame and surrounding area are dry and free of rot, mold or damage. At all four corners of the basement window, measure from the inside edges of the window frame to the wall surface. Add 1" to the longest of these measurements.

Set your table saw to make a rip cut to the width arrived at in step 1. If you don't have a table saw, set up a circular saw and straightedge cutting guide to cut strips to this length. With a fine-tooth panel-cutting blade, rip enough plywood strips to make the four jamb frame components.

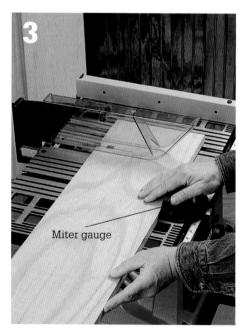

Miter gauge

Cross-cut the plywood strips to correct lengths. In our case, we designed the jamb frame to be the exact same outside dimensions as the window frame, since there was some space between the jamb frame and the rough opening.

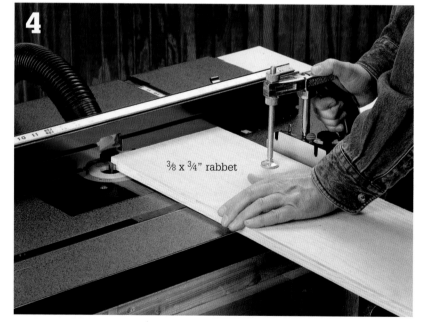

⅜ x ¾" rabbet

Cut ⅜"-deep × ¾"-wide rabbets at each end of the head jamb and the sill jamb. A router table is the best tool for this job, but you may use a table saw or hand saws and chisels. Inspect the jambs first and cut the rabbets in whichever face is in better condition. To ensure uniformity, we ganged the two jambs together (they're the same length). It's also a good idea to include backer boards to prevent tear-out.

(Continued next page)

Glue and clamp the frame parts together, making sure to clamp near each end from both directions. Set a carpenter's square inside the frame and check it to make sure it's square.

Before the glue sets, carefully drill three perpendicular pilot holes, countersunk, through the rabbeted workpieces and into the side jambs at each corner. Space the pilot holes evenly, keeping the end ones at least ¾" in from the end. Drive a 1⅝" drywall screw into each pilot hole, taking care not to overdrive. Double check each corner for square as you work, adjusting the clamps if needed.

Let the glue dry for at least one hour (overnight is better), then remove the clamps and set the frame in the window opening. Adjust the frame so it is centered and level in the opening and the exterior-side edges fit flush against the window frame.

Taking care not to disturb the frame's position (rest a heavy tool on the sill to hold it in place if you wish), press a steel rule against the wall surface and mark trimming points at the point where the rule meets the jambs at each side of all four frame corners, using a sharp pencil.

Remove the frame and clamp it on a flat work surface. Use a straightedge to connect the scribe marks at the ends of each jamb frame side. Set the cutting depth of your circular saw to just a small fraction over ¾". Clamp a straightedge guide to the frame so the saw blade will follow the cutting line and trim each frame side in succession. (The advantage to using a circular saw here is that any tear-out from the blade will be on the nonvisible faces of the frame).

Replace the frame in the window opening in the same orientation as when you scribed it and install shims until it is level and centered in the opening. Drive a few finish nails (hand or pneumatic) through the side jambs into the rough frame. Also drive a few nails through the sill jamb. Most trim carpenters do not drive nails into the head jamb.

Insulate between the jamb frame and the rough frame with spray-in polyurethane foam. Look for minimal-expanding foam labeled "window and door" and don't spray in too much. Let the foam dry for a half hour or so and then trim off the excess with a utility knife. Tip: Protect the wood surfaces near the edges with wide strips of masking tape.

Remove the masking tape and clean up the mess from the foam (there is always some). Install case molding. We used picture-frame techniques to install fairly simple oak casing.

Mechanical Systems

Adding the plumbing, wiring, and HVAC (heating, ventilation, and air conditioning) elements is one of the more challenging aspects of basement and attic remodeling. If your current systems can accommodate the added loads, you can expand them by adding new lines to provide service to the space, but making the connections and finding room for everything can be difficult. Finishing a basement means hiding all the mechanical equipment that's already in place, in addition to the new service lines. Attics are simply tough to reach, and providing service often means going through the floors and the walls in between. Considering what's involved, most homeowners seek professional guidance when planning systems expansions for attic or basement conversions.

Before you call a contractor, do some planning on your own. This section can help you get started. There's a discussion of the basic planning steps, followed by some sample projects of popular basement and attic additions. These provide an overview of typical plumbing and wiring installations, including the basic procedures for installing several fixtures. There's also a discussion of your options for heating, cooling, and ventilating your new living space.

After the planning is completed, you may decide to do some of the work yourself. Many homeowners hire professionals to handle the more difficult jobs, like adding circuits and rerouting ductwork, but complete the simpler tasks, like installing fixtures, themselves. If you plan to do your own work, check with the local building department; there may be restrictions on what jobs you can do yourself. And if you're not familiar with any of the procedures involved, make sure you get the help you need—from professionals or reference books—to do the job properly.

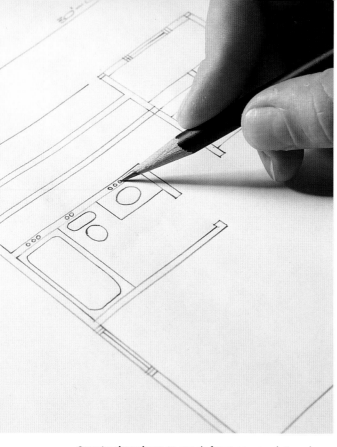

Route service lines along walls, joists, and beams so they don't limit headroom in the open area of rooms.

Check the capacity of your main systems sources to determine if the systems can support additional lines.

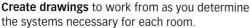

Create drawings to work from as you determine the systems necessary for each room.

Planning Your Systems

Coming up with a plan for your systems involves asking three questions about the finished space: What systems services does each room need? What sources will supply them? And how will these services be delivered? For example, to add a bathroom, determine the plumbing, electrical, heating, and ventilation requirements for the room. Then, examine your home's existing systems to see if they can be expanded to meet these requirements. And finally, find the best way to extend those services to the bathroom. You'll probably have to repeat this process for some of the rooms, so it's best to stay open to alternatives.

To find out what's needed for the room, start by choosing the types of fixtures for the bathroom and making rough plans of the overall room layout. Then, consult the local building codes. They will tell you what systems are required, such as a hard-wired vent fan and a permanent light fixture, as well as minimum room dimensions and clearances around fixtures.

When you have a general systems plan for each room, hire the appropriate contractors to assess the plans based on the existing systems

in your house. They will check the capacity of each system to determine if it can handle the additional load. For example, if your electrical service panel is nearly full, you may need to install a new subpanel to supply electricity to the new rooms.

The contractors should also help you with the next step: figuring out how to route all the pipes, wires, ducts, etc. to the new rooms. This can be tricky, and you may find it's easier to change a room layout or move a room than to move the needed systems lines. In most cases, locating an attic bathroom over an existing kitchen or bathroom greatly simplifies the plumbing hookups.

Routing the lines themselves often requires creative solutions. Think about the major issues first—ducts and drain pipes are more difficult to route than supply pipes and wiring. You can run many of the lines through and between the framing members of floors, ceilings, and walls. Be sure to follow code restrictions for notching and boring joists and studs, to maintain their structural integrity. When lines can't be hidden within framing, try to group them together so they can be enclosed in a soffit or vertical chase.

Adding a Basement Bath

When installing a basement bath, make sure you allow extra time for tearing out the concrete floor to accommodate the drains, and for construction of a wet wall to enclose supply and vent pipes. Constructing your wet wall with 2 × 6 studs and plates will provide ample room for running pipes. Be sure to schedule an inspection by a building official before you replace the concrete and cover the walls with wallboard.

Whenever possible, try to hold down costs by locating your basement bath close to existing drains and supply pipes.

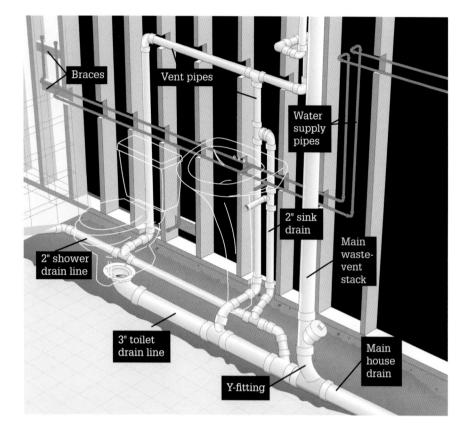

Braces Vent pipes Water supply pipes 2" sink drain Main waste-vent stack 2" shower drain line 3" toilet drain line Y-fitting Main house drain

Our demonstration bathroom includes a shower, toilet, and pedestal sink arranged in a line to simplify trenching. A 2" drain pipe services the new shower and sink; a 3" pipe services the new toilet. The drain pipes converge at a Y-fitting joined to the existing main drain. The toilet and sink have individual vent pipes that meet inside the wet wall before extending up into the attic, where they join the main waste-vent stack.

How to Plumb a Basement Bath

Outline a 24"-wide trench on the concrete where new branch drains will run to the main drain. In our project, we ran the trench parallel to an outside wall, leaving a 6" ledge for framing a wet wall. Use a masonry chisel and hand maul to break up concrete near the stack.

Use a circular saw and masonry blade to cut along the outline, then break the rest of the trench into convenient chunks with a jackhammer. Remove any remaining concrete with a chisel. Excavate the trench to a depth about 2" deeper than the main drain. At vent locations for the shower and toilet, cut 3" notches in the concrete all the way to the wall.

Cut the 2 × 6 framing for the wet wall that will hold the pipes. Cut 3" notches in the bottom plate for the pipes, then secure the plate to the floor with construction adhesive and masonry nails. Install the top plate, then attach studs.

Assemble a 2" horizontal drain pipe for the sink and shower, and a 3" drain pipe for the toilet. The 2" drain pipe includes a solvent-glued trap for the shower, a vent T, and a waste Y with 45° elbow for the sink drain. The toilet drain includes a toilet bend and a vent T. Use elbows and straight lengths of pipe to extend the vent and drain pipes to the wet wall. Make sure the vent fittings angle upward from the drain pipe at least 45°.

5

Use pairs of stakes with vinyl support straps slung between them to cradle drain pipes in the proper position. The drain pipes should be positioned so they slope ¼" per foot down toward the main drain.

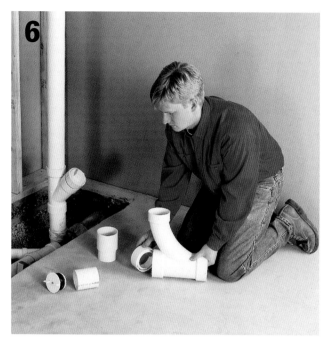

6

Assemble the fittings required to tie the new branch drains into the main drain. In our project, we will be cutting out the cleanout and sweep on the main waste-vent stack in order to install a new assembly that includes a Y-fitting to accept the two new drain pipes.

7

Support the main waste-vent stack before cutting. Use a 2 × 4 for a plastic stack, or riser clamps for a cast iron stack. Using a reciprocating saw (or a snap cutter), cut into the main drain as close as possible to the stack.

8

Cut into the stack above the cleanout and remove the pipe and fittings. Wear rubber gloves, and have a bucket and plastic bags ready, as old pipes and fittings may be coated with messy sludge.

(Continued next page)

9

Test-fit, then solvent-glue the new cleanout and reducing Y assembly into the main drain. Support the weight of the stack by adding sand underneath the Y, but leave plenty of space around the end for connecting the new branch pipes.

10

Working from the reducing Y, solvent-glue the new drain pipes together. Be careful to maintain proper slope of the drain pipes when gluing. Be sure the toilet and shower drains extend at least 2" above the floor level.

11

Check for leaks by pouring fresh water into each new drain pipe. If no leaks appear, cap or plug the drains with rags to prevent sewer gas from leaking into the work area as you complete the installation.

12

Run 2" vent pipes from the drains up the inside of the wet wall. Notch the studs and insert a horizontal vent pipe, then attach the vertical vent pipes with an elbow and vent T-fitting. Test-fit all pipes, then solvent-glue them in place.

13

Route the vent pipe from the wet wall to a point below a wall cavity running from the basement to the attic. Note: If there is an existing vent pipe in the basement, you can tie into this pipe rather than run the vent to the attic.

14

If you are running vent pipes in a two-story home, remove sections of wall surface as needed to bore holes for running the vent pipe through wall plates. Feed the vent pipe up into the wall cavity from the basement.

15

Wedge the vent pipe in place while you solvent-glue the fittings.Support the vent pipe at each floor with vinyl pipe straps. Do not patch the walls until your work has been inspected by a building official.

(Continued next page)

Cut into the main stack in the attic, and install a vent T-fitting. (If the stack is cast iron use banded couplings, and make sure to support it adequately above and below the cuts.) Attach a test T-fitting to the vent T, then join the new vent pipe to the stack, using elbows and lengths of straight pipe as needed.

Shut off the main water supply, cut into the water supply pipes as near as possible to the new bathroom, and install T-fittings. Install full-bore control valves on each line, then run ¾" branch supply pipes down into the wet wall by notching the top wall plate. Extend the pipes across the wall by notching the studs.

Use reducing T-fittings to run ½" supplies to each fixture, ending with female threaded adapters. Install backing boards, and strap the pipes in place. Attach metal protector plates over notched studs to protect pipes. After having your work approved by a building official, fill in around the pipes with dirt or sand, then mix and pour new concrete to cover the trench. Trowel the surface smooth, and let the concrete cure for three days before installing fixtures.

Installing Countertops & Sinks

Most bathroom countertops installed today are integral (one-piece) sink-countertop units made from cultured marble or other solid materials, like Corian® or Swanstone®. Integral sink-countertops are convenient, and many are inexpensive, but style and color options are limited.

Some remodelers and designers still prefer the distinctive look of a custom-built countertop with a self-rimming sink basin, which gives you a much greater selection of styles and colors. Installing a self-rimming sink is very simple.

Tools&Materials
pencil ∎ scissors ∎ carpenter's level ∎ screwdriver ∎ channel-type pliers ∎ ratchet wrench ∎ basin wrench ∎ cardboard ∎ masking tape ∎ plumber's putty ∎ lag screws ∎ tub & tile caulk

Integral sink-countertops are made in standard sizes to fit common vanity widths. Because the sink and countertop are cast from the same material, integral sink-countertops do not leak, and do not require extensive caulking and sealing.

Tips for Countertops

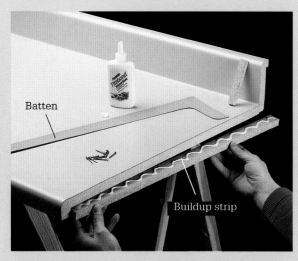

Batten

Buildup strip

Postform countertops are made from inexpensive, factory-laminated particleboard, usually with a built-in backsplash and front flange. Buildup strips and battens are used to finish the edges of the countertops, and holes for the sink basins are cut to size using a jigsaw. Countertops are held in place with corner braces and caulk.

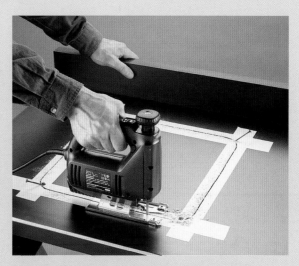

To make the sink cutout in a countertop or the backer material for a tile countertop, trace the sink cutout onto strips of masking tape on the countertop, using a sink template. Drill a starter hole just inside the outline, then carefully complete the cutout using a jigsaw. Note: Apply tape to the foot of the jigsaw to prevent scratching.

How to Install an Integral Sink-Countertop

1

Pop-up drain lever

Drain flange

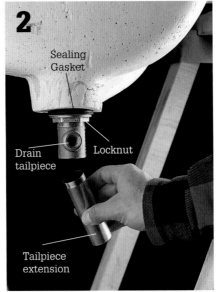

2

Sealing Gasket

Drain tailpiece

Locknut

Tailpiece extension

Thread the locknut and sealing gasket onto the drain tailpiece, then insert the tailpiece into the drain opening and screw it onto the drain flange. Tighten the locknut securely. Attach the tailpiece extension. Insert the pop-up stopper linkage.

Set the sink-countertop unit onto sawhorses. Attach the faucet, and slip the drain lever through the faucet body. Place a ring of plumber's putty around the drain flange, then insert the flange in the drain opening.

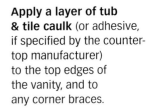

3

Apply a layer of tub & tile caulk (or adhesive, if specified by the counter-top manufacturer) to the top edges of the vanity, and to any corner braces.

Cabinets with corner braces: Secure the counter-top to the cabinet by driving a mounting screw through each corner brace and up into the countertop. Note: Cultured marble and other hard countertops require predrilling and a plastic screw sleeve.

4

Center the sink-countertop unit over the vanity, so the overhang is equal on both sides and the backsplash of the countertop is flush with the wall. Press the countertop evenly into the caulk.

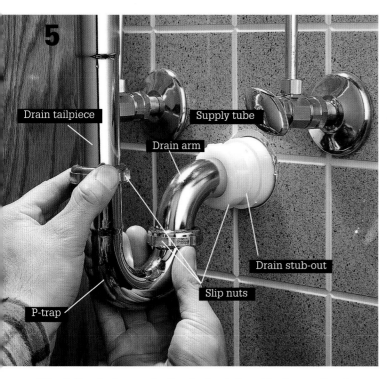

Attach the drain arm to the drain stub-out in the wall, using a slip nut. Attach one end of the P-trap to the drain arm, and the other to the tailpiece of the sink drain, using slip nuts. Connect supply tubes to the faucet tailpieces.

Seal the gap between the backsplash and the wall with tub & tile caulk. Center the sink-countertop unit over the vanity, so the overhang is equal on both sides and the backsplash of the countertop is flush with the wall. Press the countertop evenly into the caulk.

How to Install a Surface Mount Sink

Use a template that is ½" narrower than the sink rim to mark the countertop cutout. Drill a ⅜" starter hole, then use a jigsaw to make the cutout. For countertop mounted faucets, drill holes for the tailpieces, according to the faucet manufacturer's directions.

Apply a ring of plumber's putty around the sink cutout. Before setting the sink in place, attach the faucet body to the sink or countertop, and the drain flange and pop-up drain assembly.

Set the sink into the cutout area, and gently press the rim of the sink into the plumber's putty. Hook up the drain and supply fittings (step 5, above), then caulk around the sink rim.

How to Install a Pedestal Sink

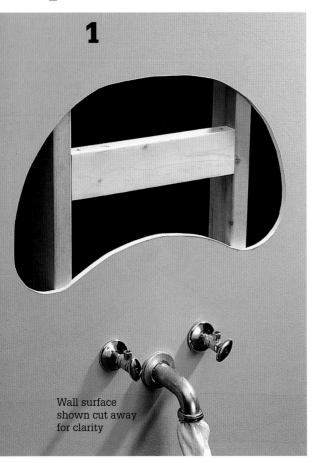

1

Wall surface
shown cut away
for clarity

Install 2 × 4 blocking between the wall studs, behind the planned sink location. Cover the wall with water-resistant drywall.

2

Set the basin and pedestal in position, bracing the basin with 2 × 4s. Outline the top of the basin on the wall, and mark the base of the pedestal on the floor. Mark reference points on the wall and floor through the mounting holes found on the back of the sink and the bottom of the pedestal.

3

Set aside the basin and pedestal. Drill pilot holes in the wall and floor at the reference points, then reposition the pedestal. Anchor the pedestal to the floor with lag screws.

4

Attach the faucet, then set the sink on the pedestal. Align the holes in the back of the sink with the pilot holes drilled in the wall, then drive lag screws and washers into the wall brace, using a ratchet wrench. Do not overtighten the screws.

5

Hook up the drain and supply fittings. Caulk between the back of the sink and the wall when installation is finished.

Installing a Toilet

Most toilets in the low-to-moderate price range are two-piece units, with a separate tank and bowl, made of vitreous china. One-piece toilets with integral tank and bowl also are available, but the cost is usually two or three times that of two-piece units.

Code regulations requiring low-flow (1.6 gallons per flush) toilets have been on the books for years. After some initial problems with inadequate flush force, manufacturers have re-engineered the toilet traps and flush mechanisms to maximize efficiency. These new models work considerably better than first-generation low-flow toilets from the 1980s to mid '90s. Most are reasonably priced and well worth the cost for eliminating aggravation (and double flushing).

Tools&**Materials** adjustable wrench ▪ ratchet wrench ▪ or basin wrench ▪ screwdriver ▪ wax ring & sleeve ▪ plumber's putty ▪ floor bolts ▪ tank bolts with rubber washers ▪ seat bolts ▪ and mounting nuts

Install a toilet by anchoring the bowl to the floor first, then mounting the tank onto the bowl. China fixtures crack easily, so use care when handling them.

How to Replace a Toilet

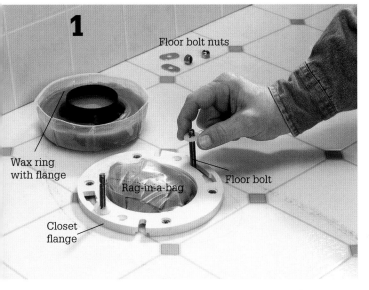

1

Floor bolt nuts

Wax ring with flange

Rag-in-a-bag

Floor bolt

Closet flange

Place a rag in a plastic sack. Slide new brass bolts into the slots on the closet flange, and rotate the bolts a ¼ turn so they cannot be removed. Put the plastic keepers or extra washers and nuts on the bolts to secure the bolts to the flange. Unwrap the wax ring and position it over the closet flange.

2

Lower the new toilet down over the wax ring so the bolts go through the holes on the bottom of the stool (this can be tricky—be patient and get help). Press down on the toilet to seat it in the wax ring and check for level. If the bowl is not quite level, you can shim the low side with a few pennies. Thread washers and nuts onto the floor bolts and tighten them a little at a time, alternating. Do not overtighten. Cut the bolts off above the nuts with a hacksaw and add the caps. Lay a bead of tub and tile caulk around the base of the toilet, but leave the back open to let water escape so you'll know if there's ever a leak.

(Continued next page)

3

Spud nut

Spud washer

Attach the toilet tank. Some tanks come with a flush valve and a fill valve preinstalled, but if yours does not, insert the flush valve through the tank opening and tighten a spud nut over the threaded end of the valve. Place a foam spud washer on top of the spud nut.

4

If necessary, adjust the fill valve as noted in the directions.

5

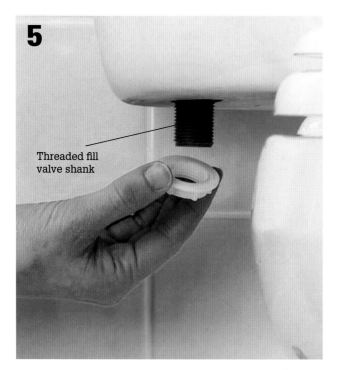

Threaded fill valve shank

Position the valve in the tank. Push down on the valve shank (not the top) while hand-tightening the lock nut onto the threaded valve shank (thread the nut on the exterior side of tank). Hand-tighten only.

6

Intermediate nut goes between tank and bowl

With the tank lying on its back, thread a rubber washer onto each tank bolt and insert it into the bolt holes from inside the tank. Then, thread a brass washer and hex nut onto the tank bolts from below and tighten them to a quarter turn past hand tight. Do not overtighten.

7

Position the tank on the bowl, spud washer on opening, bolts through bolt holes. Put a rubber washer followed by a brass washer and a wing nut on each bolt and tighten these up evenly.

8

You may stabilize the bolts with a large slotted screwdriver from inside the tank, but tighten the nuts, not the bolts. You may press down a little on a side, the front, or the rear of the tank to level it as you tighten the nuts by hand. Do not overtighten and crack the tank. The tank should be level and stable when you're done.

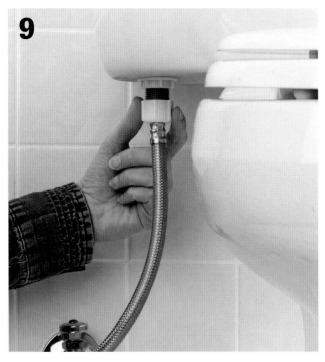

9

Hook up the water supply by connecting the supply tube to the threaded fill valve with the coupling nut provided. Turn on the water and test for leaks.

10

Attach the toilet seat by threading the plastic or brass bolts provided with the seat through the openings on the back of the rim and attaching nuts.

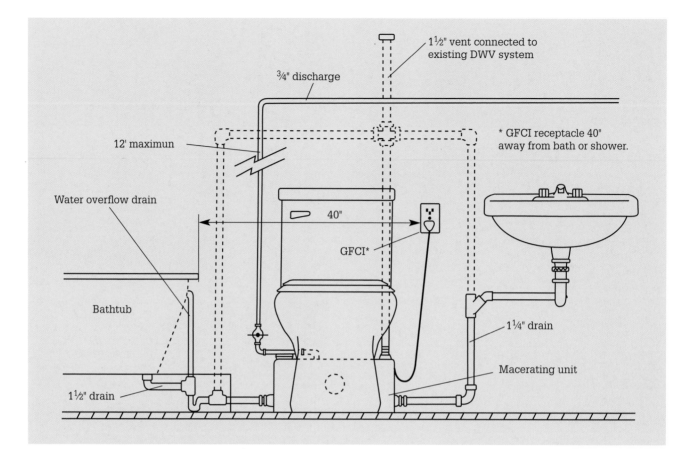

A typical macerating unit will support a toilet, a sink, a tub, and shower. This diagram shows pipe routes for a typical installation. Check local codes before installing.

Labels in diagram:
- 1½" vent connected to existing DWV system
- ¾" discharge
- 12' maximun
- * GFCI receptacle 40" away from bath or shower.
- Water overflow drain
- 40"
- GFCI*
- Bathtub
- 1¼" drain
- Macerating unit
- 1½" drain

Macerating Toilets

When a toilet with conventional plumbing is not an option, a macerating toilet may allow you to add a bathroom in a basement. Macerators grind and then eject waste through a ¾" pipe into an existing drain pipe. Most units will also handle waste water from a sink and a shower.

Place the macerating unit in the desired location and make the connections to the 1½" diameter drain lines from the sink and tub or shower to the inlets on the macerating unit. Also connect the ¾" drain line from the soil stack or a branch drain to the discharge port on the unit (you can use either copper or PVC pipe). The drain line may span up to 12 ft. vertically with some models, and it can be run as far as 150 ft. horizontally if a ¼" per-foot drop is maintained. Read the instructions carefully to learn the limits for your fixture, as well as how to factor in pressure drops that occur when the line makes a bend.

Once all connections are made at the macerating unit, place the toilet bowl in front of the unit so that the toilet spigot lines up with the accordion connector on the macerating unit. Mark the location of the toilet bowl's mounting-screw holes. Remove the toilet and drill appropriately sized holes for the toilet's mounting lag screws. Join the toilet to the macerating unit as directed by the manufacturer, and secure the toilet to the floor. The toilet tank connects to the bowl like a standard two-piece toilet. The water supply connection to the fill valve is also standard. Venting should be provided in accordance with local codes and the manufacturer's instructions.

The macerating unit must be plugged in to a 120-volt GFCI-protected outlet (the outlet should be 40" away from the unit). The unit will not function during a power outage. Do not dispose of paper products (other than toilet paper) in the macerating toilet system. Do not use bleach cakes or other submerged tank-and-bowl cleaning products.

Installing a Shower

The easiest way to build a shower is to use prefabricated shower stall panels and a plastic shower base. For a custom finish that takes a little more time, you can use ceramic tile.

Showers can be built in different sizes and configurations, but the basic elements are the same: There's a supply system, a drain system, and a framed alcove. The supply system consists of hot and cold water pipes leading to the faucet, which mixes the water and sends it up to the shower head. The drain system has a tailpiece and a P-trap that connects to the branch drain line. The alcove has 2 × 4 walls and a shower base set into a layer of mortar. Water-resistant wallboard provides adequate backing for prefab panels, but cementboard is a better backer for tile.

Frame the alcove, centering it over the drain. Add braces for the supply pipes, faucet, and shower head. Cover the framing with water-resistant wallboard.

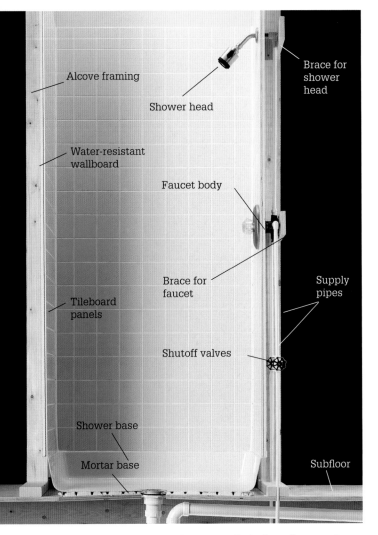

Alcove framing
Shower head
Brace for shower head
Water-resistant wallboard
Faucet body
Brace for faucet
Supply pipes
Tileboard panels
Shutoff valves
Shower base
Mortar base
Subfloor

A basic shower stall has three framed walls built to fit around a prefabricated base. In an attic bathroom, the water supply pipes usually come from underneath the floor. In a basement, they enter from a side wall.

Pour a 1" thick layer of dry-set mortar for the shower base. Set the shower base, fitting the drain tailpiece over drain pipe. Level the base, and let the mortar dry.

Prepare the shower stall panels by cutting holes for the faucet and shower head. Glue the panels to the walls, and support them with braces while the glue dries.

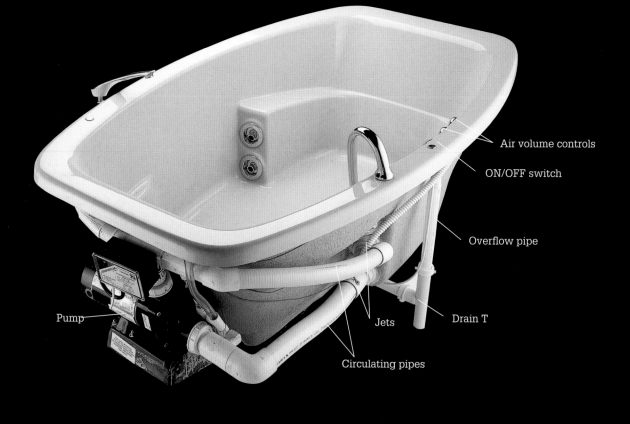

Air volume controls

ON/OFF switch

Overflow pipe

Pump

Jets

Drain T

Circulating pipes

A whirlpool circulates aerated water through jets mounted in the body of the tub. Whirlpool pumps move as much as 50 gallons of water per minute to create a relaxing "hydromassage" effect. The pump, pipes, jets, and most of the controls are installed at the factory, making the actual hookup in your home quite simple.

Installing a Whirlpool

Installing a whirlpool is very similar to installing a bathtub, once the rough-in is completed. Completing a rough-in for a whirlpool requires that you install a separate GFCI-protected electrical circuit for the pump motor. Some building codes specify that a licensed electrician be hired to wire whirlpools; check with your local building inspector.

Select your whirlpool before you do rough-in work, because exact requirements will differ from model to model. Select your faucet to match the trim kit that comes with your whirlpool. When selecting a faucet, make sure the spout is large enough to reach over the tub rim. Most whirlpools use "widespread" faucets because the handles and spout are separate, and can be positioned however you like, even on opposite sides of the tub. Most building centers carry flex tube in a variety of lengths for connecting faucet handles and spout.

Tools & Materials framing square ▪ circular saw
▪ drill & spade bits ▪ jigsaw ▪ hacksaw ▪ trowel ▪ screwdriver
▪ staple gun ▪ straightedge ▪ utility knife ▪ tiling tools ▪ caulk
gun ▪ 2 × 4 lumber ▪ 10d nails ▪ ¾" exterior-grade plywood
▪ galvanized deck screws ▪ dry-set mortar ▪ 12" wood spacer
blocks ▪ 8-gauge insulated wire ▪ grounding clamp ▪ paper-faced
fiberglass insulation ▪ cementboard ▪ ceramic tile materials
▪ silicone caulk

Optional Whirlpool Accessories

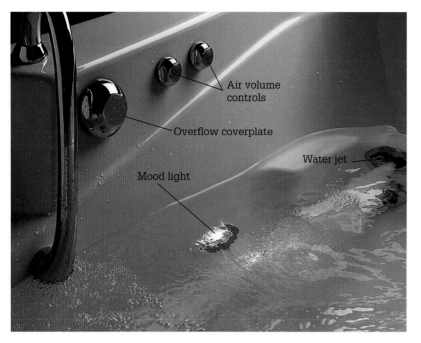

Mood lights are sold as factory-installed accessories by many manufacturers. Most are available with several filters to let you adjust the color to suit your mood. Mood lights are low-voltage fixtures wired through 12-volt transformers. Do not wire mood lights or other accessories into the electrical circuit that supplies the pump motor.

Trim kits for whirlpools are ordered at the time of purchase. Available in a variety of finishes, all of the trim pieces except the grab bar and overflow coverplate normally are installed at the factory.

Requirements for Making Electrical Hookups

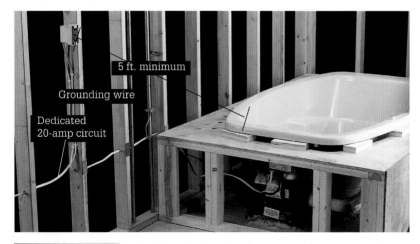

The electrical service for a whirlpool should be a dedicated 115- to 120-volt, 20-amp circuit. The pump motor should be grounded separately, normally to a metal cold water supply pipe. Most whirlpool motors are wired with 12/2 NM cable, but some local codes require the use of conduit. Remote timer switches (left), located at least 5 ft. from the tub, are required by some codes, even for a tub with a built-in timer.

A GFCI circuit breaker at the main service panel is required with whirlpool installations. Hire an electrician to connect new circuits at your service panel if you are uncomfortable installing circuit cables on your own.

How to Install a Whirlpool

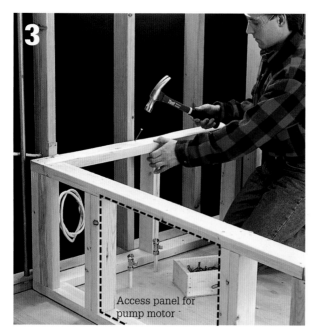

Outline the planned location of the deck frame on the subfloor. Use the plumbing stub-outs as starting points for measuring. Before you begin to build the deck, check the actual dimensions of your whirlpool tub to make sure they correspond to the dimensions listed in the manufacturer's directions. Note: Plan your deck so it will be at least 4" wide at all points around the whirlpool.

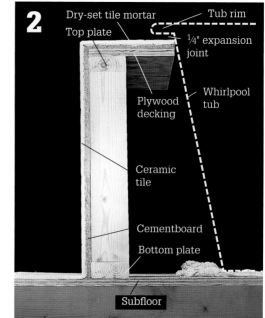

Cut top plates, bottom plates, and studs for the deck frame. The height of the frame should allow ¾" for the plywood decking, ¼" for an expansion gap between the deck and the tub rim, and 1" for cementboard, tile, and mortar.

Assemble the deck frame. Make sure to leave a framed opening for access panels at the pump location and the drain location. Nail the frame to the floor joists and wall studs or blocking, using 10d nails.

Cover the deck frame with ¾" exterior-grade plywood, and attach with deck screws spaced every 12". Using a template of the whirlpool cutout (usually included with the tub), mark the deck for cutting. If no template is included, make one from the shipping carton. (Cutout will be slightly smaller than the outside dimensions of the whirlpool rim.)

5

Drill a starter hole inside the cutout line, then make the cutout hole in the deck, using a jigsaw.

6

Measure and mark holes for faucet tailpieces and spout tailpiece according to the faucet manufacturer's suggestions. Drill holes with a spade bit or hole saw.

7

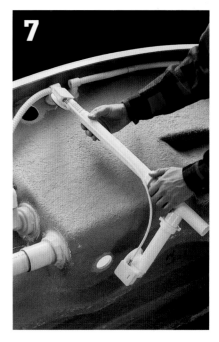

Attach drain-waste-overflow assembly (included with most whirlpools) at the drain and overflow outlets in the tub. Trim the drain pipe in the floor to the proper height, using a hacksaw.

8

Apply a layer of dry-set mortar to the subfloor where the tub will rest. Make 12" spacer blocks, 1¼" thick (equal to expansion gap, tile mortar, and cementboard; see step 2). Arrange blocks along the edges of the cutout.

9

With a helper, lift the tub by the rim and set it slowly into the cutout hole. Lower the tub, pressing it into the mortar base, until the rim rests on the spacers at the edges of the cutout area. Align the tailpiece of the drain-waste-overflow assembly with the P-trap as you set the tub in place. Avoid moving or shifting the tub once it is in place, and allow the mortar to set for 6 to 8 hours before proceeding with the tub installation.

(Continued next page)

Adjust the length of the tailpiece for the drain-waste-overflow assembly, if necessary, then attach assembly to the P-trap in the drain opening, using a slip nut.

Inspect the seals on the built-in piping and hoses for loose connections. If you find a problem, contact your dealer for advice. Attempting to fix the problem yourself could void the whirlpool warranty.

With the power off, remove the wiring cover from the pump motor. Feed the circuit wires from the power source or wall timer into the motor. Connect the wires according to the directions printed on the motor.

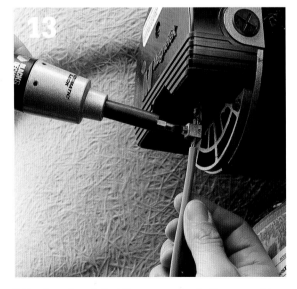

Attach an insulated 8-gauge wire to the ground lug on the pump motor.

Attach the other end of the wire to a metal cold water supply pipe in the wall, using a ground clamp. Test the GFCI circuit breaker.

Clean out the tub, then fill it so the water level is at least 3" above the highest water jet.

Turn on the pump, and allow it to operate for at least 20 minutes while you check for leaks. Contact your whirlpool dealer if leaks are detected.

Staple paper-faced fiberglass insulation to the vertical frame supports. The facing should point inward, to keep fibers out of motor. Do not insulate within 6" of pumps, heaters, or lights.

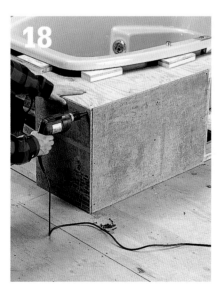

Attach cementboard to the sides and top of the deck frame if you plan to install ceramic tile on the deck. Use ¾" plywood for access panel coverings.

Attach finish surfaces to deck and deck frame, then install grab bar, faucet, and spout. Fill the joints between the floor and deck, and between the tub rim and deck surface, with silicone caulk.

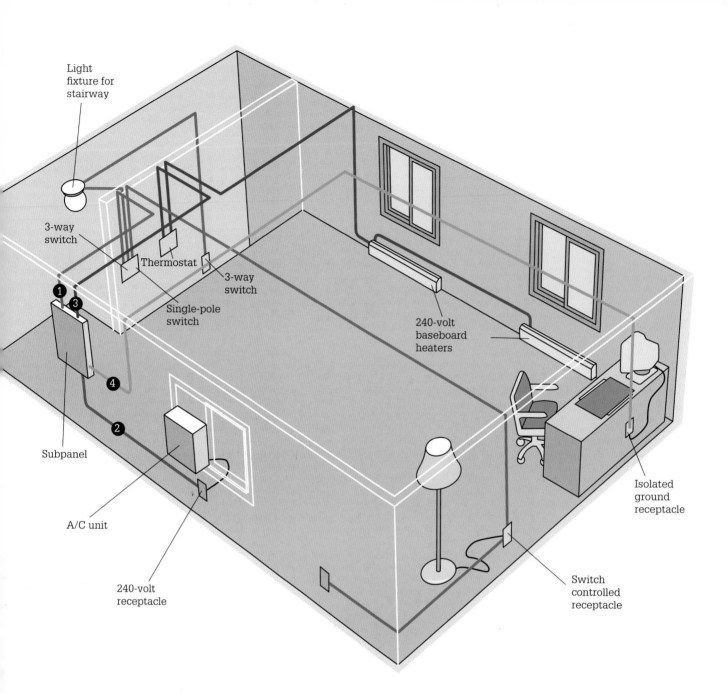

Light fixture for stairway

3-way switch

Thermostat

3-way switch

Single-pole switch

240-volt baseboard heaters

① ③

Subpanel

④

②

A/C unit

240-volt receptacle

Isolated ground receptacle

Switch controlled receptacle

(Above) Map out electrical circuits for your room. The circuits for this attic room start at a subpanel, which is powered by the main servicepanel. *Circuit 1* controls the room's lighting and standard receptacles. *Circuit 2* feeds a 20-amp, 240-volt receptacle for a window air conditioner. *Circuit 3* is also a 240-volt circuit, providing power to a thermostat and two baseboard heater units. *Circuit 4* feeds an isolated ground receptacle for computer equipment. Circuits 2, 3, and 4 are dedicated circuits, meaning each serves only one device or series of heaters. See pages 86 to 87 for a closer look at these wiring layouts.

Draw plans that include all devices required by local codes.

Run extra wiring for computer, TV, speaker, and phone connections.

Wiring a Room

Your plans for wiring a room addition should reflect the ways you will use the space. For example, an attic sitting area should have a receptacle for an air conditioner, while a basement sewing room will need plenty of lighting. To determine your electrical needs, think about the finish space and the types of fixtures you plan to include. Also, consult the local building department to make sure your plans comply with local codes. The following are some of the basic electrical elements to consider.

The National Electrical Code requires receptacles to be spaced no more than 12 ft. apart, but for convenience you can space them as close as 6 ft. apart. You may need some non-standard receptacles, such as a GFCI (for bathrooms and wet areas), a 20-amp or 240-volt receptacle (for large appliances), and an isolated-ground receptacle (for a computer). Also consider the placement of furniture in the finished room; avoid placing receptacles or baseboard heaters where they may be blocked by furniture.

Lighting is an important consideration for every room, particularly rooms with limited sources of ambient light. Most codes require that each room have at least one switch-controlled light fixture, with the switch placed near the room's entrance. Stairways must have lighting that illuminates each step, and the fixture must be controlled by three-way switches at the top and bottom landings. Hallways and closets also need switch-controlled lights. In addition to meeting code requirements, your lighting plan should include different types of lighting to provide versatility for everyday tasks, as well as visual warmth. This is especially true in basements, which generally need more artificial light than upper floors. It helps to use plenty of indirect lighting to eliminate shadows and provide ambient background light.

Your basement or attic rooms will also probably need additional wiring to supply auxiliary HVAC equipment. A typical bathroom vent fan or a ceiling fan runs on a standard 120-volt circuit, while most window air conditioners and baseboard heaters require 240-volt circuits. If you'll be installing an electric radiant heating system for supplemental heat, find out what type of circuit wiring the system requires.

One way to avoid long wiring runs and crowding of the main service panel is to install a circuit breaker subpanel in or near the finished space. A subpanel gets its power supply from a single cable leading from the main panel. With adequate amperage, a subpanel can serve all of the circuits necessary for the finished space—all from a convenient location.

Finally, don't forget the wiring that's not connected directly to the electrical panel, such as telephone lines and jacks, special cables for Internet access, speaker wiring, and coaxial cable for television and video connections. During a finishing project, it pays to run extra wiring for these types of connections. The minor expense of running additional wiring now will be more than offset by the convenience of having the wiring in place if you need it in the future. For coaxial cable and other communications wiring, be sure to maintain the recommended clearances from electrical cable, to avoid electrical interference.

Employ several different types of lighting to create an effective lighting scheme. Recessed, track, and under-cabinet light fixtures illuminate this basement with an attractive blend of lighting effects.

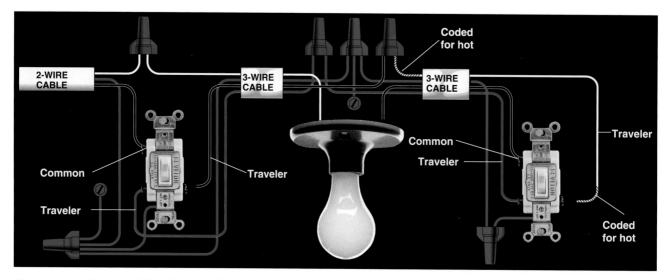

Three-way switches and light fixture: This configuration lets you control a light fixture from two locations. Each switch has one common terminal and two traveler terminals. Circuit wires attached to the traveler screws run between the switches. Hot wires attached to the common screws power the fixture.

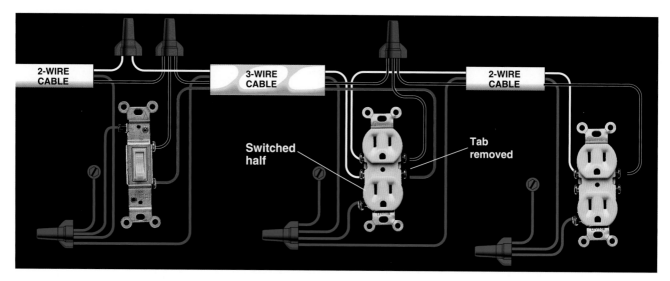

Switch-controlled split receptacle, duplex receptacle: This layout lets you use a switch to control a lamp plugged into a receptacle. Only the bottom half of the first receptacle is controlled by the switch; the remaining receptacle outlets are always hot. This configuration requires two-wire and three-wire cables.

Wiring Diagrams

These diagrams show you the wiring configurations for the circuits found in the attic-room illustration on page 162. They include many of the common devices and wiring layouts for a basic wiring plan.

In these examples, the power sources for the circuits are supplied by a subpanel. The black wires in the diagrams are "hot," meaning they carry voltage; the white wires are "neutral," or zero-voltage, unless they are marked "coded for hot". The red wires in three-wire cables are used in different configurations

to make hot, neutral, or ground connections. The green wires represent ground wires, each of which terminates at a grounding screw. In actual wiring, grounding wires are usually bare copper. Grounding screws are required in all metal electrical boxes, but plastic boxes do not need to be grounded.

The circuit cables represented in each configuration are standard non-metallic cable. The 240-volt circuits use 12-gauge cable; all other circuits are 15-amp and use 14-gauge cable.

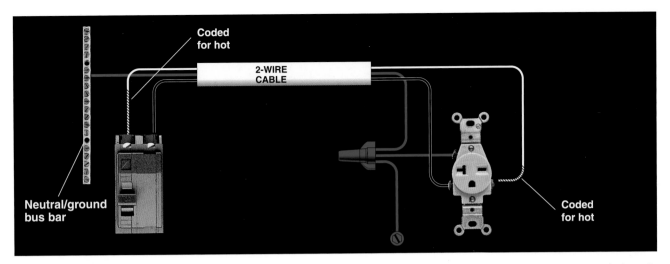

240-volt appliance receptacle: This layout includes a 20-amp, 240-volt dedicated appliance circuit that services a window air conditioner. The black and white circuit wires connected to a double-pole breaker each bring 120 volts of power to the receptacle. 12-gauge cable is used to accommodate the 20-amp current.

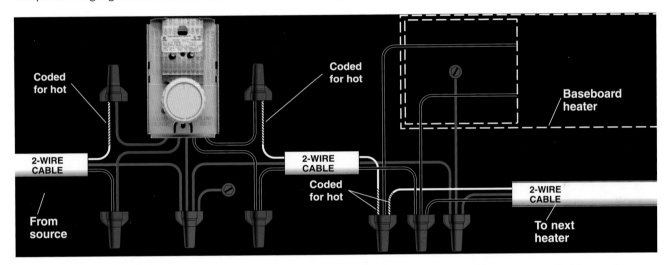

240-volt baseboard heaters: This configuration is typical for a series of 240-volt baseboard heaters controlled by a wall thermostat. All heaters in the circuit are wired as shown, except for the last heater, which is connected to only one cable. The circuit and cable sizes are determined by the total wattage of the heaters.

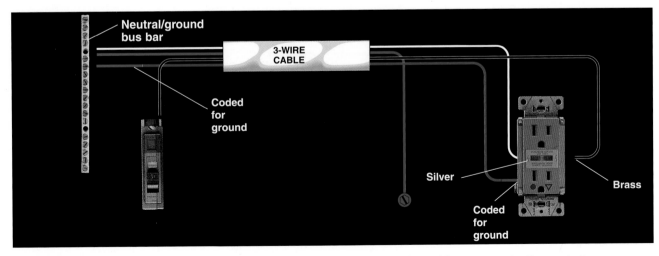

Dedicated 120-volt computer circuit, isolated ground receptacle: This circuit provides extra protection against power surges. The red wire in a three-wire cable serves as an extra grounding conductor, connecting the grounding screw on an isolated ground receptacle directly to the grounding bus bar in the subpanel.

Incandescent Light Fixture

Standard incandescent light fixtures are attached permanently to ceilings or walls. They include wall-hung sconces, ceiling-hung globe fixtures, and chandeliers. Most types are easy to install using basic tools.

Incandescent fixtures must mount to an electrical box that is attached either to the framing directly or by means of a metal brace that spans framing cavities. Wiring for most fixtures is simple. A two-wire circuit cable—with a black hot wire, a white neutral wire, and a ground wire—enters the box and is affixed by a cable clamp. The fixture itself has permanently attached wire leads for each light socket. To install the fixture, connect the wire leads to the circuit wires, using wire connectors, then mount the fixture to the box.

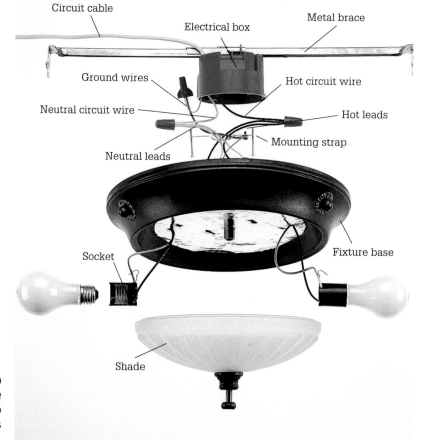

Circuit cable · Electrical box · Metal brace · Ground wires · Hot circuit wire · Neutral circuit wire · Hot leads · Mounting strap · Neutral leads · Fixture base · Socket · Shade

Incandescent light fixtures connect to the house circuit with pre-installed wire leads. Fixtures are secured directly to electrical boxes or to mounting straps attached to the boxes.

Installation Overview: Incandescent Light Fixture

Grounding screw

Attach a fixture mounting strap to the electrical box, if the box does not already have one. The strap may have a preinstalled grounding screw.

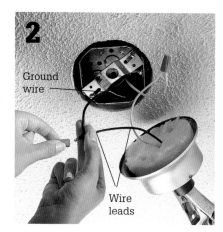

Ground wire

Wire leads

Using wire connectors, connect the white wire lead to the white circuit wire, and the black lead to the black circuit wire. Attach the ground wire to the grounding screw on the mounting strap.

Attach the fixture base to the mounting strap, using the screws provided. Install a light bulb with a wattage rating consistent with the fixture rating, then attach the fixture globe.

Recessed Light Fixtures

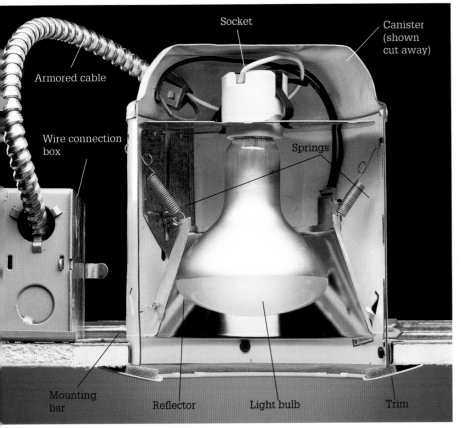

Socket

Canister (shown cut away)

Armored cable

Wire connection box

Springs

Mounting bar

Reflector

Light bulb

Trim

Recessed light fixtures are housed in metal canisters that mount flush with the ceiling finish material. Each fixture has its own wire connection box where the connections to the house circuit are made.

Recessed light fixtures are especially popular for basement and attic finishing projects because they don't compromise valuable headroom.

You can mount recessed fixtures inside framed soffits or between ceiling joists, or you can attach them to a suspended ceiling grid. When attaching the fixtures to framing, install the fixtures and complete the wiring connections during the rough-in stage, before you install the wallboard or other ceiling material.

If your fixtures will be housed within an insulated ceiling, make sure they are rated IC (insulated ceiling), so that you can insulate up to and over the fixtures. Standard fixtures need 3" of clearance from any insulation. Always use IC fixtures in attic ceilings.

Installation Overview: Mounting a Recessed Light Fixture to Framing

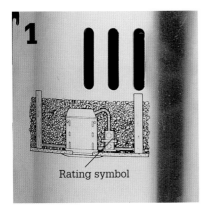

1

Rating symbol

Check the fixture's insulation rating. If the ceiling or soffit containing the fixtures will be insulated, make sure the fixtures are rated for insulated ceilings (IC).

2

Extend the fixture's mounting bars to reach the framing members, aligning the bars with the bottom faces of the framing. Drive the pointed ends of the bars into the framing.

3

Remove the wire connection box cover and open one knockout for each cable entering the box. Install a cable clamp for each open knockout.

Track Lighting

Track lighting is the most versatile type of permanent lighting. The tracks can be installed in any direction along walls and ceilings, and the fixtures can easily be moved anywhere along the track. A variety of styles of track lighting units are available in kits.

One advantage of track lighting is that an entire system can be powered by a single electrical box. The first track mounts over the box and is connected to the circuit wiring. Additional tracks are mounted to the ceiling and are tied into the first track with *L-connectors* or *T-connectors*. The lighting fixtures are individual units that connect to the tracks at any location.

Install the tracks and fixtures after the ceiling finish is in place. For the best effect, place tracks parallel to the wall closest to the fixture.

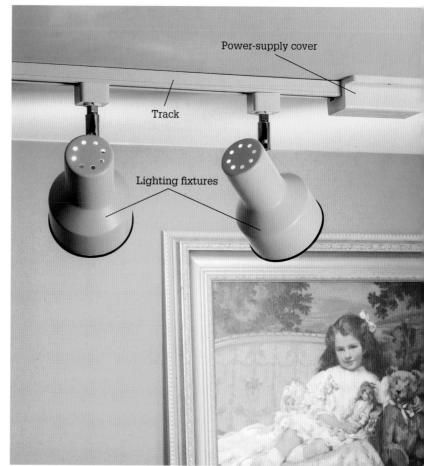

Track lighting makes it easy to create custom lighting effects. The individual fixtures can be arranged to highlight art work, provide focused task lighting, or supply indirect lighting to brighten a dark corner.

Installation Overview: Track Lighting

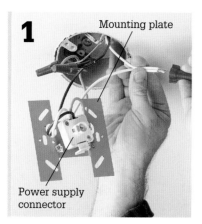

1

Mounting plate

Power supply connector

Connect the power-supply connector to the circuit wires, using wire connectors. Then, attach the mounting plate to the electrical box.

2

Power supply connector

Mount the first track to the ceiling, screwing it into framing members or using toggle bolts. Secure the track to the mounting plate with screws. Snap the power-supply connector into the track.

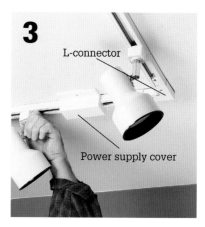

3

L-connector

Power supply cover

Install additional tracks, connecting them to the first track with L- or T-connectors. Install the power-supply cover. Cap bare trackends with dead-end pieces. Position the light fixtures as desired.

Baseboard Heaters

A baseboard heater is a simple electrical unit consisting of a heating element with attached metal fins for transferring heat and a *limit control*—a switch that prevents the element from overheating. To control temperature, some models have built-in thermostats; others are controlled by wall mounted thermostats that are wired directly to the heaters.

Typically a baseboard heater and its thermostat are hard-wired to a 240-volt circuit. In these circuits, both the black and white circuit wires are hot. Other types of heaters use only 120 volts. These may be hard-wired to a household circuit or plugged into a standard receptacle.

For best results, position baseboard heaters along outside walls, beneath windows.

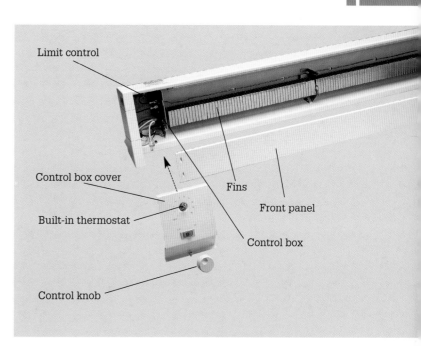

Limit control
Control box cover
Built-in thermostat
Control knob
Fins
Front panel
Control box

Baseboard heaters have control boxes that house the wiring. Units with control boxes at both ends usually can be wired at either end. Hard-wired heaters are often controlled by a wall-mounted thermostat.

Installation Overview: Baseboard Heater (hard-wired)

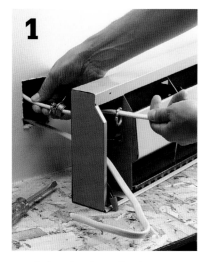

1

Feed the circuit cables into the connection box, and secure them with cable clamps. If there is more than one heater in the circuit, there will be two cables.

2

Position the heater against the wall, about 1" off the floor, and anchor it to the wall studs with screws. Strip away the cable sheathing so at least ¼" of sheathing extends into the connection box.

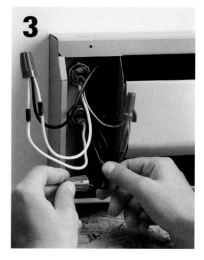

3

Make the wire connections with wire connectors, following the manufacturer's wiring diagram. For 240-volt circuits, tag the white wires with black tape to indicate they are hot. Install the box cover.

Ventilating Attics

Windows and skylights provide effective, passive ventilation for attics. Opening the windows in the attic and the first floor of the house encourages natural circulation of cool air up through the floors. Whenever possible, install windows on opposing walls to create a cross-breeze when both windows are open. Room air conditioners also can help ventilate an attic by replacing stale indoor air with outdoor air. However, a single unit may not provide adequate ventilation for an entire attic. Check with the local building department for ventilation requirements in your area.

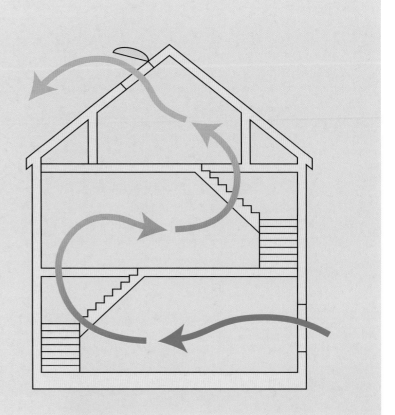

Radiant Heating Systems

Radiant heating systems come in many forms, but there are two general types: hydronic and electric. Hydronic systems use hot water—heated and circulated by a gas boiler—that flows through plastic or rubber tubing. One common installation method is to staple the tubing to the underside of the subfloor, which heats the floor above (photo, top right). Another method is to set the tubing in a new slab of lightweight concrete. This can be a good option for heating basement floors if there's enough headroom to accommodate the new slab.

Electric systems are more versatile than hydronic systems and are great for providing heat to specific areas. For example, an electric mat system is designed to heat tiled floors. The heating mats can be installed directly over a concrete floor or over cementboard on wood floors. A layer of thin-set tile adhesive is troweled over the mat, and the tile is set into the adhesive (photo, bottom right). The whole system is powered by a household circuit and controlled by a thermostat and timer.

Providing Heating & Cooling

There are many options for supplying heat and air conditioning to your basement or attic. You can expand your home's central system, add a new system, or simply install some auxiliary heating or cooling appliances.

Expanding a forced-air system in a basement usually requires only a few added ducts. Running ducts to the attic is more challenging: often the easiest method is to extend a duct straight up through the intermediate floors of the house. You can conceal the new ducts in closets and other inconspicuous areas or frame and finish a small wall around them. A hydronic (water or steam) heating system can be expanded by adding new pipes and fixtures; this is a job for a plumber or mechanical contractor.

The main concern is whether your HVAC system can handle the additional load. If it cannot, and an upgraded furnace or boiler doesn't fit your budget, consider more localized supplemental units, such as electric baseboard heaters and room air conditioners. Both use normal household current and are controlled by their own thermostats, which provide better temperature control for specific rooms than a remote whole-house thermostat.

Room A/C units typically plug into a 240-volt receptacle, while heaters either plug into a standard 120-volt receptacle or are hard-wired to a 240-volt circuit (see page 165). Either may require a new circuit in your electrical panel.

A gas fireplace is another good source of supplemental heat, and today's direct-vent fireplaces can be installed in almost any room. *Heater* models are designed to reach higher temperatures than standard models, and units with electric fans circulate warm air into the living space more efficiently.

Radiant heating systems are an increasingly popular option for remodels. These systems provide heat via electrical wires or hot-water tubing laid out in a ribbon pattern behind the finish surfaces of walls, ceilings, and floors. Radiant systems can supply dry, consistent heat to warm anything from a tiled floor in a half-bath to an entire basement slab. Large-scale radiant installations, however, are not for do-it-yourselfers.

In addition to mechanical systems, nature also plays a significant role in heating and cooling your home. Surrounded by earth, basements maintain a consistently cool temperature throughout the year, and in many climates need little or no air conditioning. Attics are just the opposite: they collect all the warm air that rises from the rooms below and can be difficult to cool. The natural ventilation provided by windows and skylights goes a long way to keeping attics comfortable during warm months.

Room air conditioners can be installed in windows or wall openings. Their cooling power is measured in Btus, and it's important to get a properly sized unit for the space it's cooling. For help with determining your cooling needs, contact the Association of Home Appliance Manufacturers.

Electric baseboard heaters are a good option for rooms that need only supplemental or occasional heating. For best results, place them along exterior walls and under windows, and provide an open space in front of the unit for air circulation.

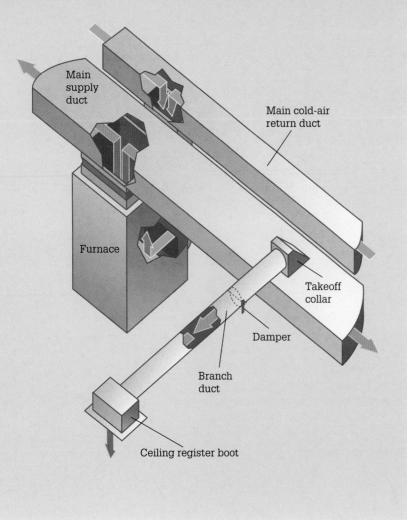

Main supply duct

Main cold-air return duct

Furnace

Takeoff collar

Damper

Branch duct

Ceiling register boot

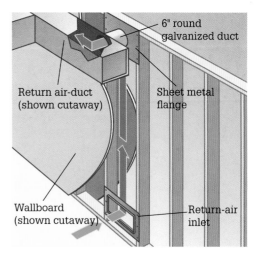

6" round galvanized duct

Return air-duct (shown cutaway)

Sheet metal flange

Wallboard (shown cutaway)

Return-air inlet

Cold-air return ducts often consist of enclosed stud or joist cavities with an air inlet at one end and a boot or fitting at the other end that feeds into a branch duct. The cavities may be enclosed with wallboard or subflooring, or with flat metal sheeting nailed to the framing members. To ensure adequate air flow, the cavity should not hold plumbing or blocking, but a few wires are usually acceptable.

Forced-Air Systems

A typical gas-furnace forced-air system has a main *supply* duct leading from the furnace and extending across the basement space just under the joists of the floor above. This duct supplies the warm air to the entire house via a network of *branch* ducts. The *return* ducts are just the reverse: They bring cool air from the rooms back to the furnace, providing air circulation throughout the house. (To find out which is which, turn on the furnace and feel the ducts: Supply ducts will be warm, return ducts cool.) The whole system is balanced by adjustable *dampers* located inside the branch ducts and controlled by the home's thermostat.

Some systems—called *zone systems*—are balanced by several automatic dampers. Each damper is controlled by its own thermostat,

thus maintaining a consistent temperature within a specific zone. Zone systems are complicated, and you'll need the help of an HVAC specialist to expand the system.

With standard systems, providing heat and air conditioning to remodeled spaces is fairly straightforward. While you're planning the walls and thinking about which rooms are going where, have an HVAC specialist take a look at your system. He or she can help you find the best way to distribute air to the new space without compromising service to the rest of the house.

In most cases, you can run new branch ducts directly from the main supply duct or from another branch duct and use empty wall-stud cavities to serve as branch cold-air return ducts.

Installation Overview: Branch Supply Duct

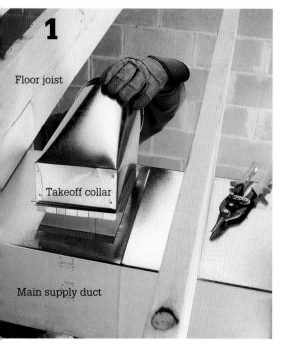

1

Floor joist

Takeoff collar

Main supply duct

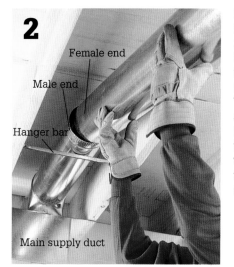

2

Female end

Male end

Hanger bar

Main supply duct

Run the branch duct out to the register boot location (see step 3). Starting from the main duct, install full sections of duct by fitting their plain female ends over their crimped male ends. The crimped ends should point away from the main duct. Use hanger bars or straps to support the sections temporarily as you work. Fasten the sections together with two sheet metal screws.

Attach a starting collar to the main duct. A takeoff collar mounts to the top or side of the main duct; a straight collar mounts to the side. Cut a hole into the duct to accept the tabbed end of the collar, using aviation snips. Fit the collar in the hole, then secure it by bending over the tabs inside the duct. Secure two of the tabs with self-tapping sheet metal screws.

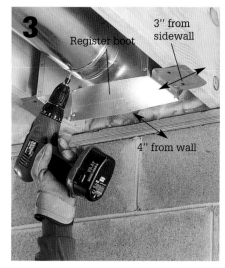

3

Register boot

3" from sidewall

4" from wall

Install the register boot, then attach the final duct section. Position the boot so that the long side is at least 4" from the room's long wall and the short side is at least 3" from any side wall. Mount the boot to the joists. If you need to shorten the final section of duct, cut from the plain end, and use a connecting band, if necessary, to join the last two duct sections. Attach the final section to the boot with screws. Install permanent hanger bars or straps every 4 to 6 ft. along the duct.

DIY Tip ▶ Here are a few tips to help you with the planning

- Plan branch ducts with as few turns as possible; air moves most efficiently through short, straight runs of duct.
- Round, galvanized metal duct is the most efficient for moving air, while flexible duct is about the least. Use flexible duct only where metal isn't practical. To save space, you may be able to use shallow rectangular metal duct that fits between studs and joists.
- Locate supply registers near exterior walls, below or above windows, if possible. Include at least one in each room. Place return air inlets on walls opposite the supply registers, to draw heated or cooled air across the space. To avoid circulating moist and odorous air through the system, do not place cold-air return inlets in bathrooms or kitchens.
- To get an idea of the size of branch ducts you'll need, examine the existing ductwork. Note the sizes and lengths of the branch ducts and the dimensions of the rooms they serve, then compare those with the new space.
- If possible, run ducts inside clear joist cavities. Where ducts must run beneath joists, route them through closets (or behind kneewalls in attics), to minimize the number of soffits necessary to conceal them.

Finishing Walls & Ceilings

At this stage in the remodeling project, much of the heavy work is done. You've completed the framing and rough-ins, and now it's time to install insulation and cover everything up with finish materials. It's a satisfying process to transform the skeletal maze of framing into clearly defined rooms, and your success with this step will not only affect the look of your finished rooms, but will also help determine how comfortable they will be throughout the seasons.

Insulating is an easy, if unpleasant, chore that most people do themselves, but it's important to complete this job properly. You'll need to find out what insulating techniques work best in your area. For example, houses in some climates must have vapor barriers installed over the insulation to keep moisture from rotting the framing. And roof insulation is especially important in cold regions, where finishing an attic can create problems if the roof is not effectively insulated and ventilated. You may also want to insulate your floors, ceilings, and interior walls for soundproofing.

After the insulation comes the fun job of deciding what materials you'll use to finish the walls and ceilings. Wallboard is the most common finish used by do-it-yourself remodelers. It's inexpensive and easy to install, and it provides a smooth, flat surface for paint or wallcoverings. Tongue-and-groove paneling is a bit more challenging to install, but the result is a warm, natural-wood finish that you can't get with wallboard. The paneling project in this section shows you a basic installation procedure that you can apply to different paneling treatments. A popular choice for basement projects is a suspended ceiling, which is particularly suitable for an informal room. A suspended ceiling makes it easy to cover the many service lines running through a basement, and it provides quick access to shutoff valves and drain cleanouts.

But before you cover your walls and ceiling with any material, make sure you have the approval from the building inspector on everything that lies within them; you won't want to tear down your newly finished wallboard because the inspector didn't check your wiring staples.

Handling fiberglass is a lot less uncomfortable when you're dressed for it. Wear pants and a long-sleeve shirt, gloves, goggles, and a good-quality dust mask or respirator. Shower as soon as you finish the installation.

Fiberglass insulation comes in *batts* cut to length for standard stud-wall bays as well as long rolls. Various options include: kraft-paper and foil facings, which serve as vapor barriers (some foils are flame-resistant); plastic-encapsulated blankets; high density blankets (for rafters); and standard, unfaced rolls and batts. Standard widths fit between 16"- and 24"-on-center framing.

Installing Insulation

Before you insulate your basement or attic (or even buy insulation), ask the local building department about two things: *R-value* and *vapor barriers*. All insulation has an R-value clearly printed on its packaging. This is the measure of how well the insulation keeps in the heat and keeps out the cold, and vice versa. The higher the R-value, the better the insulation works—and the thicker it is. The building department will tell you what R-values you need for your walls and ceilings, and whether the insulation job must be inspected before you cover it.

Vapor barriers come in a few different forms, but all have a common purpose. They prevent the water vapor present in warm indoor air from passing beyond the wall or ceiling surface and through the framing, where it contacts cold exterior surfaces and condenses. This condensation promotes mildew growth that can rot the framing and insulation. Vapor barriers are required in most seasonal climates and are typically installed on the "warm-in-winter" side of exterior walls and attic ceilings, between the insulation and the interior finish material.

Paper- and foil-faced and encapsulated insulation have their own vapor barriers, but for a more effective, continuous barrier, use a layer of 6-mil polyethylene sheeting stapled to framing members over unfaced insulation. Also be aware that faced insulation comes with a few drawbacks. The paper tears easily, and facings make it difficult to cut around obstacles. And, if you trim a batt to fit into a narrow bay, you lose the facing flange—and thus, the vapor seal—on one side. Also, most facings are flammable and must be covered with wallboard or other approved finish, even in unfinished areas, such as storage rooms. One alternative is to use insulation with an approved flame-resistant foil facing.

The most important part of insulating is making sure there are no gaps between the insulation and framing, around obstructions, or between insulation pieces. The idea is to create a continuous "thermal envelope" that keeps interior air from contacting outdoor temperatures.

Tools & Materials Utility knife ▪ stapler ▪ Fiberglass insulation ▪ 6-mil polyethylene sheeting ▪ staples ▪ packing tape

Insulate around pipes, wires, and electrical boxes by peeling the blanket in half and sliding the back half behind the obstruction. Then, lay the front half in front of the obstruction. Cut the front half to fit snugly around boxes.

Use scraps of insulation to fill gaps around window and door jambs. Fill the cavities loosely to avoid compressing the insulation. Fill narrow gaps with expanding spray-foam insulation, following manufacturer's instructions.

Never compress insulation to fit into a narrow space. Instead, use a sharp utility knife to trim the blanket about ¼" wider and longer than the space. To trim, hold the blanket in place and use a wall stud as a straightedge and cutting surface.

How to Install Vapor Barriers

Provide a vapor barrier using faced insulation by tucking along the edges of the insulation until the facing flange is flush with the edge of the framing. Make sure the flanges lie flat, with no wrinkles or gaps, and staple them to the faces of the framing members about every 8". Patch any gaps or facing tears with packing tape or a construction tape supplied by the manufacturer.

Install a polyethylene vapor barrier by draping the sheeting over the entire wall or ceiling, extending it a few inches beyond the perimeter. Staple the sheeting to the framing, and overlap sheets at least 12". Carefully cut around obstructions. Seal around electrical boxes and other penetrations with packing tape. Trim excess sheeting along the ceiling and floor after you install the finish material.

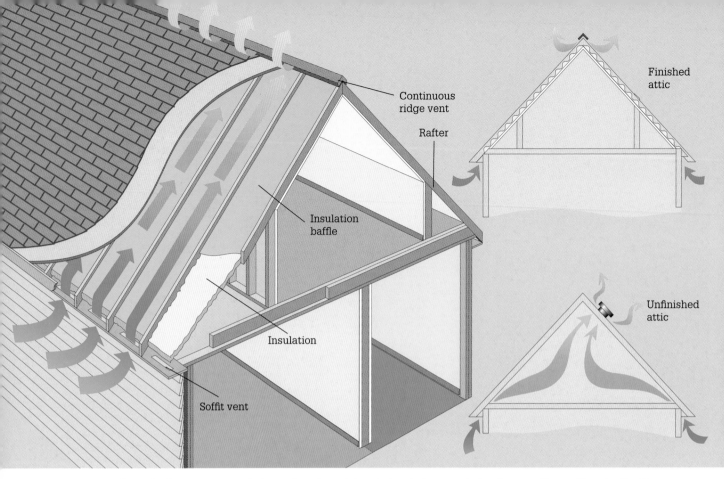

Labels in illustration:
- Continuous ridge vent
- Rafter
- Insulation baffle
- Insulation
- Soffit vent
- Finished attic
- Unfinished attic

A roof ventilation system works in conjunction with attic insulation: Insulation forms a thermal barrier that keeps in the home's conditioned air, while the ventilation system uses outdoor air to keep the roof deck cool and dry. In most unfinished attics, the entire attic space is ventilated, and proper air flow can be achieved with roof vents or gable-wall vents.

Insulating & Ventilating Roofs

Ventilation works in concert with insulation to keep your roof deck healthy. Roofs need ventilation for a number of reasons. During hot weather, direct sunlight can heat a roof considerably, and air flow underneath the roof deck helps lower temperatures, keeping your attic cooler. In cold climates, and particularly in areas with heavy snowfall, roofs need ventilation to prevent ice dams and other moisture problems. As you insulate your attic ceiling, you need to make sure the roof will remain properly ventilated.

Here's how roof ventilation works: Air intake vents installed in the soffits—called *soffit* vents—allow outdoor air to pass under the roof sheathing and flow up toward the ridge, where it exits through one or more exhaust vents. In unfinished attics, with insulation only along the floor, air is allowed to flow from open rafter bays into a common air space under the roof. It can then be exhausted through any of the roof or gable vents. When you finish your attic, however,

you enclose part or all of each rafter bay with insulation and a ceiling finish. A flat attic ceiling will provide some open air space above the ceiling, but air flow still may be limited. With a peaked ceiling, the rafter bays are enclosed up to the ridge, and a single roof vent can serve only one rafter bay. To improve ventilation, you can install additional roof and soffit vents or a continuous ridge vent, which provides ventilation to all of the rafter bays.

A roof ventilation system must have a clear air path between the intake and exhaust vents. For this reason, most building codes call for 1" of air space between the insulation and the roof sheathing. To ensure this air space remains unobstructed, install insulation baffles in the rafter bays. Also be sure to install enough insulation to meet the recommended R-value for your area. This may require increasing the depth of your attic rafters to accommodate the insulation and baffles.

Use insulation baffles to provide a continuous air channel behind the insulation. The baffles should start just in front of the exterior walls' top plates and extend up to the vents. Attach the baffles to the roof sheathing with staples.

Lay fiberglass insulation, stopping short of the baffle opening to avoid restricting air flow. Insulation in the attic floor should cover the exterior walls' top plates but not extend into the soffit cavities.

Increase the rafter depth to make room for thicker insulation by attaching 2 × 2s to the rafter edges. Fasten the 2 × 2s with 3"-long, countersunk screws. You can also save space by using high-density insulation.

Options for Ventilating Roofs

Continuous ridge vents are the most effective roof vents, because they ventilate along the entire ridge. It costs less to have one installed during a re-roofing project, but they can be installed onto an existing roof that's in good condition. This type of vent works best when used in conjunction with continuous soffit vents (below).

Roof vents (box or mushroom type) are commonly used to ventilate unfinished attics. You can improve ventilation by adding more roof vents and soffit vents (above, right). If your rafter bays are enclosed all the way to the ridge, be sure the soffit vents and roof vents are installed along the same rafter bays.

Soundproofing Walls & Ceilings

In making homes quieter, building professionals add soundproofing elements to combat everything from the hum of appliances to the roar of airliners. Many of the techniques they use are simple improvements involving common products and materials. What will work best in your home depends upon a few factors, including the types of noises involved, your home's construction, and how much remodeling you have planned. For starters, it helps to know a little of the science behind sound control.

Sound is created by vibrations traveling through air. Consequently, the best ways to reduce sound transmission are by limiting airflow and blocking or absorbing vibrations. Effective soundproofing typically involves a combination of methods.

Stopping airflow—through walls, ceilings, floors, windows, and doors—is essential to any soundproofing effort. (Even a 2-ft.-thick brick wall would not be very soundproof if it had cracks in the mortar.) It's also the simplest way to make minor improvements. Because you're dealing with air, this kind of soundproofing is a lot like weatherizing your home: Add weatherstripping and door sweeps, seal air leaks with caulk, install storm doors and windows, etc. The same techniques that keep out the cold also block exterior noise and prevent sound from traveling between rooms.

After reducing airflow, the next level of soundproofing is to improve the sound-blocking qualities of your walls and ceilings. Engineers rate soundproofing performance of wall and ceiling assemblies using a system called Sound Transmission Class, or STC. The higher the STC rating, the more sound is blocked by the assembly. For example, if a wall is rated at 30 to 35 STC, loud speech can be understood through the wall. At 42 STC, loud speech is reduced to a murmur. At 50 STC, loud speech cannot be heard through the wall.

Standard construction methods typically result in a 28 to 32 STC rating, while soundproofed walls and ceilings can carry ratings near 50. To give you an idea of how much soundproofing you need, a sleeping room at 40 to 50 STC is quiet enough for most people; a reading room is comfortable at 35 to 40 STC. For another gauge, consider the fact that increasing the STC rating of an assembly by 10 reduces the perceived sound levels by 50%. The chart on page 181 lists the STC ratings of several wall and ceiling assemblies.

Improvements to walls and ceilings usually involve increasing the mass, absorbancy, or resiliency of the assembly; often, a combination is best. Adding layers of drywall increases mass, helping a wall resist the vibrational force of sound (⅝" fire-resistant drywall works best because of its greater weight and density). Insulation and soundproofing board absorb sound. Soundproofing board is available through drywall suppliers and manufacturers (see page 235). Some board products are gypsum-based; others are lightweight fiberboard. Installing resilient steel channels over the framing or old surface and adding a new layer of drywall increases mass, while the channels allow the surface to move slightly and absorb vibrations. New walls built with staggered studs and insulation are highly effective at reducing vibration.

In addition to these permanent improvements, you can reduce noise by decorating with soft materials that absorb sound. Rugs and carpet, drapery, fabric wall hangings, and soft furniture help reduce atmospheric noise within a room. Acoustical ceiling tiles effectively absorb and help contain sound within a room but do little to prevent sound from entering the room.

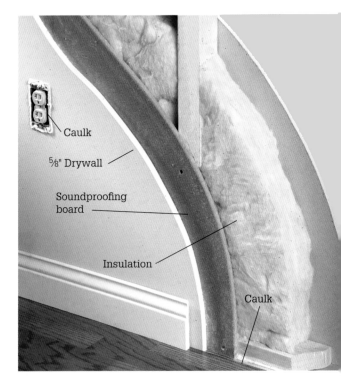

Caulk

⅝" Drywall

Soundproofing board

Insulation

Caulk

Adding soundproofing board and insulation are among the many simple ways you can reduce noise in your home.

STC Ratings for Various Wall & Ceiling Constructions*

Assembly	STC Rating	Assembly	STC Rating
Wood-frame Walls		**Steel-frame Walls**	
■ 2 × 4 wall; ½" drywall on both sides; no caulk	30	■ 3⅝" metal studs, spaced 24" on-center; ⅝" fire-resistant drywall on both sides	40
■ 2 × 4 wall; ½" drywall on both sides; caulked	35	■ 3⅝" metal studs, spaced 24" on-center, ½" fire-resistant drywall single layer on one side, doubled on other side; insulated	48
■ 2 × 4 wall; ½" drywall on both sides; additional layer of ⅝" fire-resistant drywall on one side	38	■ 2½" metal studs, spaced 24" on-center; soundproofing board (base layer) and ½" fire-resistant drywall on both sides; insulated	50
■ 2 × 4 wall; ½" drywall on both sides; additional layer of ⅝" fire-resistant drywall on both sides	40		
■ 2 × 4 wall; ½" drywall on both sides; insulated	39	**Wood-frame Floor/Ceiling**	
■ Staggered-stud 2 × 4 wall; ⅝" fire-resistant drywall on each side; insulated	50	■ Drywall below; subfloor and re-silient (vinyl) flooring above	32
■ 2 × 4 wall, soundproofing board (base layer) and ⅝" fire-resistant drywall on each side; insulated	50	■ ⅝" fire-resistant drywall attached to resilient steel channels below; subfloor, pad, and carpet above	48
■ 2 × 4 wall with resilient steel channels on one side; ⅝" fire-resistant drywall on both sides; insulated	52	■ Double layer ⅝" fire-resistant drywall attached to resilient steel channels below; subfloor, pad, and carpet above	Up to 60

*All assemblies are sealed with caulk, except where noted. Ratings are approximate.

DIY Tip ▸ Reducing Exterior Noise

Add storm doors and windows to minimize air leaks and create an additional sound barrier. Use high-performance (air-tight) storm units and maintain a 2" air gap between the storm and the primary unit.

(Above) Install weatherstripping on doors and windows to seal off any air leaks. If the wall framing around the door or window is exposed, make sure all cavities are filled with loosely packed insulation.

(Right) Seal around pipes, A/C service lines, vents, and other penetrations in exterior walls, using expanding foam or caulk. Make sure through-wall A/C units are well-sealed along their perimeters.

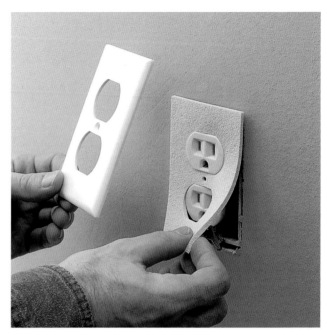

Stop airflow between rooms by sealing the joints where walls meet floors. With finished walls, remove the shoe molding and spray insulating foam, acoustic sealant, or non-hardening caulk under the baseboards. Also seal around door casings. With new walls, seal along the top and bottom plates.

Cover switch and receptacle boxes with foam gaskets to prevent air leaks. Otherwise, seal around the box perimeter with acoustic sealant or caulk and seal around the knockout where the cables enter the box.

Soundproof doors between rooms by adding a sweep at the bottom and weatherstripping along the stops. If doors are hollow-core, replacing them with solid-core units will increase soundproofing performance. Soundproof workshop and utility room doors with a layer of acoustical tiles.

Reduce sound transmission through ductwork by lining ducts with special insulation. If a duct supplying a quiet room has a takeoff point close to that of a noisy room, move one or both ducts so their takeoff points are as distant from each other as possible.

How to Install Resilient Steel Channels

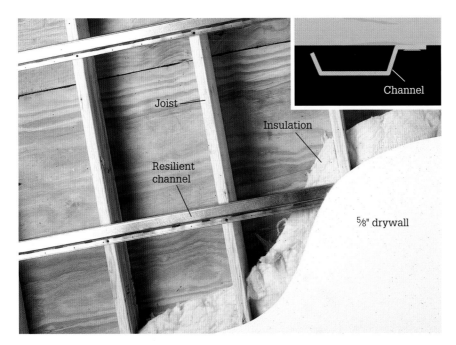

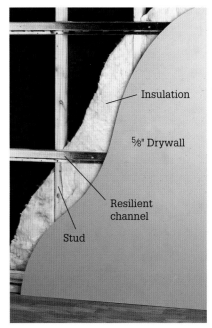

On ceilings, install channels perpendicular to the joists, spaced 24" on-center. Fasten at each joist with 1¼" type W drywall screws, driven through the channel flange. Stop the channels 1" short of all walls. Join pieces on long runs by overlapping the ends and fastening through both pieces. Insulate the joist bays with R-11 unfaced fiberglass or other insulation and install ⅝" fire-resistant drywall, run perpendicular to the channels. For double-layer application, install the second layer of drywall perpendicular to the first.

On walls, use the same installation techniques as with the ceiling application, installing the channels horizontally. Position the bottom channel 2" from the floor and the top channel within 6" of the ceiling. Insulate the stud cavities and install the drywall vertically.

How to Build Staggered-stud Partition Walls

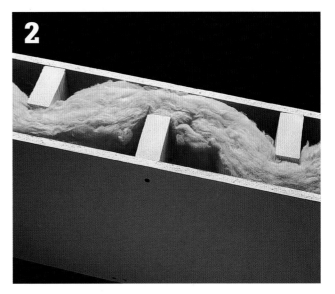

Frame new partition walls using 2 × 6 plates. Space the studs 12" apart, staggering them so alternate studs are aligned with opposite sides of the plates. Seal under and above the plates with acoustic sealant.

Weave R-11 unfaced fiberglass blanket insulation horizontally between the studs. Cover each side with one or more layers of ⅝" fire-resistant drywall.

Installing & Finishing Wallboard

Wallboard is commonly available in 4 × 8-ft. and 4 × 12-ft. panels, in thicknesses ranging from ¼" to ¾". The panels are tapered along their long edges so that adjoining panels form a slightly recessed seam that you finish with paper tape and wallboard compound. End-to-end joints are more difficult to finish, so avoid end-butted seams whenever possible. And to minimize the number of joints that need finishing, use the longest panels you can safely handle; just make sure you can get them into the workspace.

Use ½"- or ⅝"-thick panels on ceilings. Thinner panels are lighter and easier to work with, but ⅝" wallboard provides better sound insulation and is less likely to sag over time. Use ½" panels on walls. Install wallboard on the ceiling first, then finish the walls, butting the wall panels snug against the ceiling panels to give them extra support.

Tools&Materials
Wallboard T-square ▪ utility knife ▪ jig saw ▪ wallboard compass ▪ chalk line ▪ rented wallboard lift ▪ drill or screwgun ▪ lifter ▪ 4-ft. level ▪ 4", 6", 10" and 12" wallboard knives ▪ pole sander ▪ Wallboard ▪ 1¼" wallboard screws ▪ compound ▪ joint tape ▪ corner bead ▪ sandpaper

How to Cut Wallboard

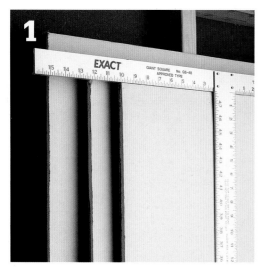

To make vertical cuts, set the wallboard panel against a wall with the front side facing out. Mark the desired length on the face, then position a wallboard T-square at the mark. Hold the square in place with your hand and foot, and cut through the face paper, using a utility knife.

Bend the scored section backwards with both hands to break the gypsum core of the wallboard. Fold back the unwanted piece, and cut through the back paper with the utility knife.

Tip: Make horizontal cuts by extending a tape measure to the desired width of the cut, and hooking a utility knife blade under the end of the tape. Grip the tape tightly in one hand and the utility knife in the other, and move both hands along the panel to cut through the face paper.

Tips for Preparing Walls and Ceilings for Wallboards

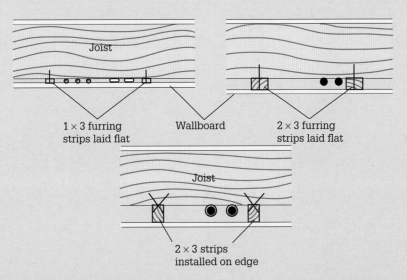

1 × 3 furring strips laid flat

Wallboard

2 × 3 furring strips laid flat

Joist

2 × 3 strips installed on edge

Attach furring strips to framing where service lines and other obstacles project beyond the framing. The strips create a flat surface for attaching wallboard. Use 1 × 3 or 2 × 3 furring strips and attach them perpendicular to the framing, using wallboard screws. Space the strips 16" or 24" on-center so that they provide support for all of the wallboard edges.

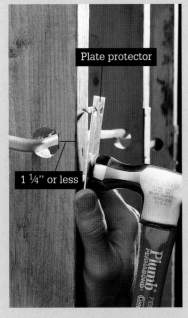

Plate protector

1 ¼" or less

Use protector plates where wires or pipes pass through framing members and are less than 1¼" from the front edge. The plates prevent wallboard screws from puncturing wires or pipes.

Make square internal cuts, such as openings for electrical boxes, using a jigsaw fitted with a coarse wood-cutting blade or a wallboard keyhole saw. To start the cut, set the base of the saw on the panel and pivot the saw downward until the blade cuts through the panel, then finish the cut with the base flat against the panel.

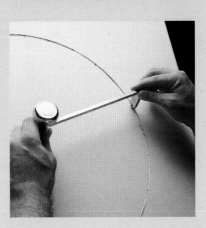

Make circular cutouts using a wallboard compass. Mark the centerpoint of the cutout, then set the point of the compass on the mark. Press down and rotate the compass to score through the paper. Tap a nail through the centerpoint to mark the other side. Score the back-side paper, then knock out the hole through front side with a hammer.

How to Install Wallboard on a Ceiling

Create a control line by measuring out from the top plate of the adjoining wall. Make a mark on the outermost joists (or rafters) at 48⅛", then snap a chalk line through the marks. The line should be perpendicular to the joists. Use the control line to align the first row of panels and to measure for cutouts.

Measure across the joists to make sure the first panel will break on the center of a joist. If necessary, cut the panel from the end that abuts the side wall so that the panel breaks on the next farthest joist. Load the panel onto a rented wallboard lift, and hoist the panel until it rests flat against the joists.

Position the panel so the side edge is even with the control line and the leading end is centered on a joist. Fasten the panel using 1¼" wallboard screws. Drive a screw every 8" along the edges and every 12" in the field (consult the local building department for fastening requirements in your area).

After the first row of panels is installed, begin the next row with a half-panel of wallboard. This ensures that the butted end joints will be staggered between rows.

How to Install Wallboard on Walls

Plan the wallboard placement so there are no joints at the corners of doors or windows. Wallboard joints at corners often crack or cause bulges that interfere with window and door trim.

Install wallboard panels vertically unless the panels are long enough to span the wall sideways. Lift the panels tight against the ceiling with wallboard lifter. Plumb the first panel with a 4-ft. level, making sure the panel breaks on the center of a stud.

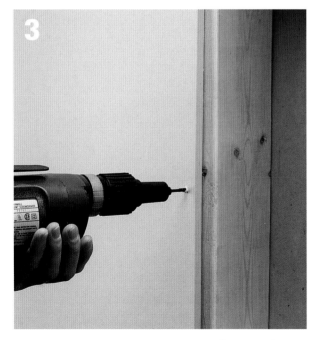

Anchor the panels to the framing with 1¼" wallboard screws. Drive a screw every 8" along the edges and every 12" in the field of the panel. Drive the screws so their heads are just below the surfaces of the panels, creating a slight depression in the face paper without breaking through it.

Tip: Unsupported wallboard edges tend to crack and sag, ruining your finishing work. When installing new wallboard next to an existing wall surface, or where the framing layout does not coincide with the wallboard edges, you may need to add 1 × or 2 × lumber backing to support wallboard edges.

How to Tape Wallboard Joints

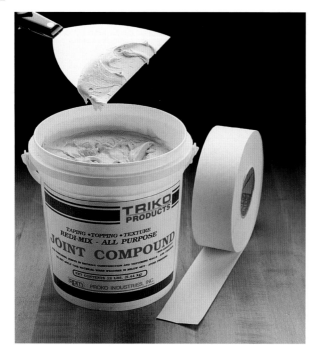

Tip: Use premixed wallboard compound for most taping and finishing jobs to eliminate messy mixing and lumpy results. When using premixed compound, also use paper wallboard joint tape.

1

Apply a thin layer of wallboard compound over the joint with a 4" or 6" wallboard knife. Load the knife by dipping it into a wallboard mud pan filled with wallboard compound.

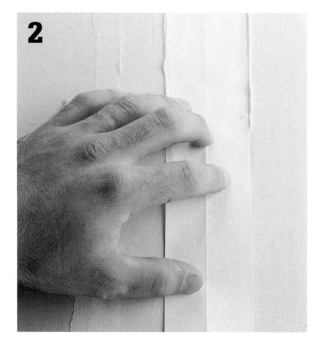

2

Press the wallboard tape into the compound immediately, centering the tape over the joint. Smooth over the tape firmly with the 6" knife to flatten the tape and squeeze out excess compound from behind it. Let the compound dry completely.

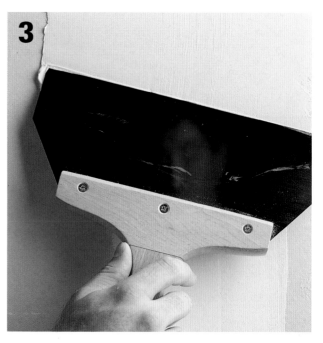

3

Apply two thin finish coats of compound with a 10" or 12" wallboard knife. Allow the second coat to dry and shrink overnight before applying the final coat. Let the final coat dry completely before sanding.

How to Finish Inside Corners

1

2

Fold a strip of paper wallboard tape in half by pinching the strip and pulling it between your thumb and forefinger.

Apply a thin layer of wallboard compound to both sides of the inside corner, using a 4" or 6" wallboard knife. Position the end of the folded tape strip at the top of the joint and press the tape into the wet compound with the knife. Smooth both sides of the corner to flatten the tape and remove excess compound. Apply two finish coats of compound.

How to Finish Outside Corners

1

2

3

Position metal corner bead on the outside corners, making sure the bead is centered along the corner. Attach the bead with 1¼" wallboard nails or screws spaced 8" apart.

Cover the corner bead with three coats of wallboard compound, using a 6" or 10" wallboard knife. Let each coat dry and shrink overnight before applying the next coat. Sand the final coat smooth.

Tip: Sand the finished joints lightly after the wallboard compound dries, using a pole sander and wallboard sandpaper or a sanding sponge. Wear a dust mask and goggles when sanding.

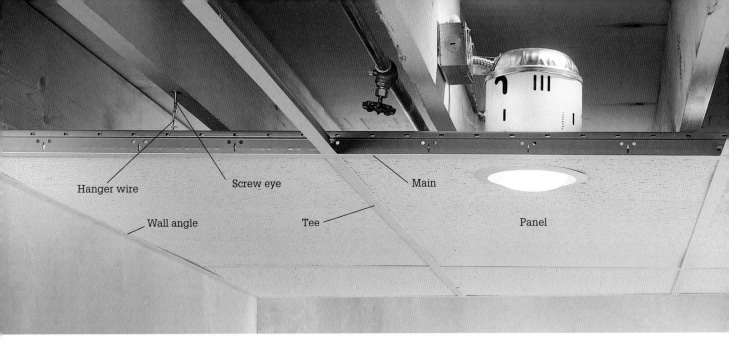

Labels on image: Hanger wire, Screw eye, Main, Wall angle, Tee, Panel

Suspended ceilings are great for basements because they provide access to mechanicals and are easy to install over uneven joists. You can also install recessed or fluorescent light fixtures that mount flush to the ceiling surface.

Installing a Suspended Ceiling

Suspended ceilings have some advantages over standard ceiling finishes (such as wallboard). Because all of the panels can be removed, virtually everything behind a suspended ceiling, like plumbing runs, shut-off valves, and wiring, is easily accessible. Also, suspended ceilings can compensate for uneven joists.

One notable disadvantage of suspended ceilings is that they take up headroom. Typically, suspended ceilings should hang about 4" below the lowest obstacle, to leave enough room for installing or removing the panels. So, before you decide on using a suspended system, measure to determine the finished ceiling height and make sure it will comply with the local building code.

A suspended ceiling is a grid framework made of lightweight metal brackets hung on wires attached to ceiling or floor joists. The frame consists of T-shaped main beams (mains) and cross-tees (tees), and L-shaped wall angles. The grid supports ceiling panels that rest on the flanges of the framing pieces. Ceiling panels come in 2 × 2-ft. or 2 × 4-ft. sections. They're available in a variety of styles, including insulated

panels, acoustical tiles that dampen sound, and light-diffuser panels that are used with fluorescent light fixtures. Generally, metal-frame ceiling systems are more durable than ones made of plastic.

To begin your ceiling project, determine the panel layout based on the width and length of the room. Often, some panels must be cut to accommodate the room. Place trimmed panels on opposite sides of your ceiling for a balanced look, as when installing floor tile or ceramic wall tile. You'll also want to install your ceiling so it's perfectly level. An inexpensive but effective tool for marking a level line around a room perimeter is a water level. You can make a water level by purchasing two water-level ends (available at hardware stores and home centers) and attaching them to a standard garden hose.

Although suspended ceilings work well for hiding mechanicals in a basement, it looks best if you build soffits around low obstructions, such as support beams and large ducts. Finish the soffits with wallboard, and install the ceiling wall angle to the soffit.

Tools & Materials water level ▪ chalk line ▪ drill ▪ screw-eye driver ▪ aviation snips ▪ dryline ▪ lock-type clamps ▪ pliers ▪ straightedge, utility knife ▪ suspended ceiling kit (frame) ▪ screw eyes, hanger wires ▪ ceiling panels, ▪ 1½" wallboard screws or masonry nails

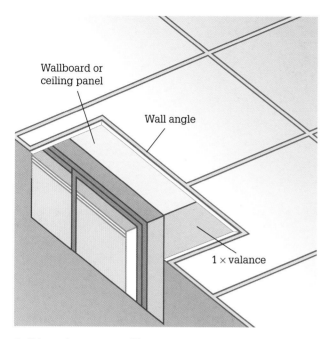

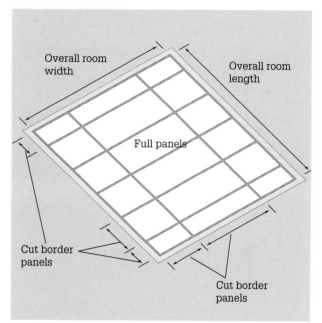

Build a valance around basement awning windows so they can be opened fully. Attach 1 × lumber of an appropriate width to joists or blocking. Install wallboard (or a suspended-ceiling panel trimmed to fit) to the joists inside the valance.

Draw your ceiling layout on paper, based on the exact dimensions of the room. Plan so that trimmed border panels on opposite sides of the room are of equal width and length (avoid panels smaller than ½-size). If you include lighting fixtures in your plan; make sure they follow the grid layout.

How to Install a Suspended Ceiling

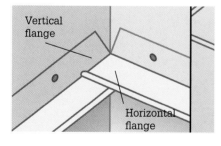

Make a mark on one wall that indicates the ceiling height plus the height of the wall angle. Use a water level to transfer that height to both ends of each wall. Snap a chalk line to connect the marks. This line indicates the top of the ceiling's wall angle.

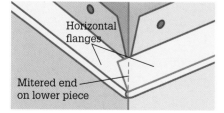

Tip: Trim wall angle pieces to fit around corners. At inside corners (top), back-cut the vertical flanges slightly, then overlap the horizontal flanges. At outside corners (bottom), miter-cut one horizontal flange, and overlap the flanges.

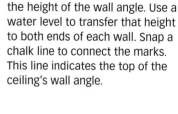

Attach wall angle pieces to the studs on all walls, positioning the top of the wall angle flush with the chalk line. Use 1½" wallboard screws (or short masonry nails driven into mortar joints on concrete block walls). Cut angle pieces using aviation snips.

(Continued next page)

3

4

Install screw eyes for hanging the mains, using a drill and screw-eye driver. Drill pilot holes and drive the eyes into joists every 4 ft., locating them directly above the guide strings. Attach hanger wire to the screw eyes by threading one end through the eye and twisting the wire on itself at least three times. Trim excess wire, leaving a few inches of wire hanging below the level of the guide string.

Mark the location of each main on the wall angles at the ends of the room. The mains must be parallel to each other and perpendicular to the ceiling joists. Set up a guide string for each main, using a thin dryline and lock-type clamps. Clamp the strings to the opposing wall angles, stretching them very taut so there's no sagging.

5

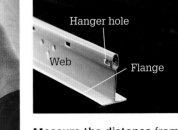

Hanger hole

Web

Flange

Measure the distance from the bottom of a main's flange to the hanger hole in the web (inset). Use this measurement to prebend each hanger wire. Measure up from the guide string and make a 90° bend in the wire, using pliers.

6

7

Tee slot

Trim one end of each main so that a tee slot in the main's web is aligned with the tee guide string, and the end of the main bears fully on a wall angle. Set the main in place to check the alignment of the tee slot with the string.

Following your ceiling plan, mark the placement of the first tee on opposite wall angles at one end of the room. Set up a guide string for the tee, using a dryline and clamps, as before. This string must be perpendicular to the guide strings for the mains.

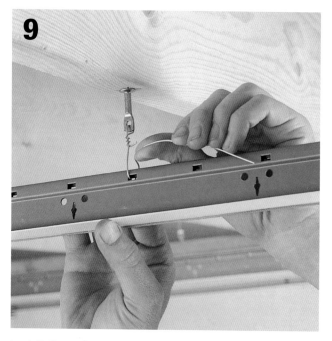

8

Cut the other end of each main to fit, so that it rests on the opposing wall angle. If a single main cannot span the room, splice two mains together, end-to-end (the ends should be fashioned with male-female connectors). Make sure the tee slots remain aligned when splicing.

9

Install the mains by setting the ends on the wall angle and threading the hanger wires through the hanger holes in the webs. The wires should be as close to vertical as possible. Wrap each wire around itself three times, making sure the main's flange is level with the main guide string. Also install a hanger near each main splice.

10

Attach tees to the mains, slipping their tabbed ends into the tee slots on the mains. Align the first row of tees with the tee guide string; install the remaining rows at 4-ft. intervals. If you're using 2 × 2-ft. panels, install 2-ft. cross-tees between the midpoints of the 4-ft. tees. Cut and install the border tees, setting the tee ends on the wall angles. Remove all guide strings and clamps.

11

Place full ceiling panels into the grid first, then install the border panels. Lift the panels in at an angle, and position them so they rest on the frame's flanges. Reach through adjacent openings to adjust the panels, if necessary. To trim the border panels to size, cut them face-up, using a straightedge and a utility knife .

Paneling an Attic Ceiling

Tongue-and-groove paneling offers a warm, attractive finish that's especially suited to the angles of an attic ceiling. Pine is the most common material for tongue-and-groove paneling, but you can choose from many different wood species and panel styles. Panels are typically ⅜" to ¾" thick and are often attached directly to ceiling joists and rafters. Some building codes require the installation of wallboard as a fire stop behind ceiling paneling that's thinner than ¼".

When purchasing your paneling, get enough material to cover about 15% more square footage than the actual ceiling size to allow for waste. Since the tongue portions of panels slip into the grooves of adjacent pieces, square footage for paneling is based on the *reveal*. The reveal is the exposed face of the panels after they are installed.

Tongue-and-groove boards can be attached with flooring nails or finish nails. Flooring nails hold better because they have spiraled shanks, but they tend to have larger heads than finish nails. Whenever possible, drive the nails through the base of the tongue and into the framing. This is called *blind-nailing,* because the groove of the succeeding board covers the nail heads. Add face-nails only at joints and in locations where more support is needed, such as along the first and last boards. And to ensure clean cuts, use a compound miter saw. These saws are especially useful for ceilings with non-90° angles.

Layout is crucial to the success of a paneling project. Before you start, measure and calculate to see how many boards will be installed, using the reveal measurement. If the final board will be less than 2" wide, trim the first, or *starter,* board by cutting the long edge that abuts the wall. If the ceiling peak is not parallel to the side (starting) wall, you must compensate for the difference by ripping the starter piece at an angle. The leading edge of the starter piece, and every piece thereafter, must be parallel to the peak.

Tools & Materials
chalk line ▪ compound miter saw ▪ circular saw ▪ drill ▪ nail set ▪ tongue-and-groove paneling ▪ 1¾" spiral flooring nails ▪ trim molding

How to Panel an Attic Ceiling

To plan your layout, first measure the reveal of the boards—the exposed surface when they are installed. Fit two pieces together and measure from the bottom edge of the upper board to the bottom edge of the lower board. Calculate the number of boards needed to cover one side of the ceiling by dividing the reveal dimension into the overall distance between the top of one wall and the peak.

Use the calculation from step 1 to make a control line indicating the top of the first row of panels. At both ends of the ceiling, measure down from the peak an equal distance, and make a mark to represent the top (tongue) edges of the starter boards. Snap a chalk line through the marks.

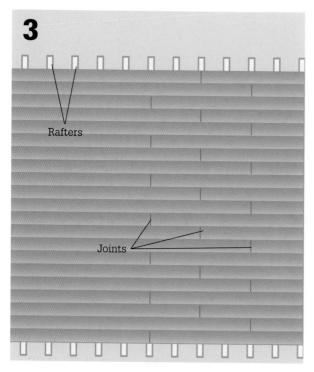

If the boards aren't long enough to span the entire ceiling, plan the locations of the joints. Staggering the joints in a three-step pattern will make them less conspicuous. Note that each joint must fall over the middle of a rafter. For best appearance, select boards of similar coloring and grain for each row.

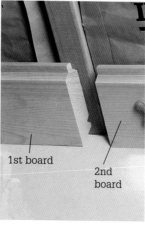

Rip the first starter board to width by bevel-cutting the bottom (grooved) edge. If the starter row will have joints, cut the board to length using a 30° bevel cut on the joint-end only. Two beveled ends joined together form a scarf joint , which is less noticeable than a butt joint. If the board spans the ceiling, square-cut both ends.

(Continued next page)

Position the first starter board so the grooved (or cut) edge butts against the side wall and the tongue is aligned with the control line. Leave a ⅛" gap between the square board end and the end wall. Fasten the board by nailing through its face about 1" from the grooved edge and into the rafters. Then, blind-nail through the base of the tongue into each rafter, angling the nail backwards at 45°. Drive the nail heads beneath the wood surface, using a nail set.

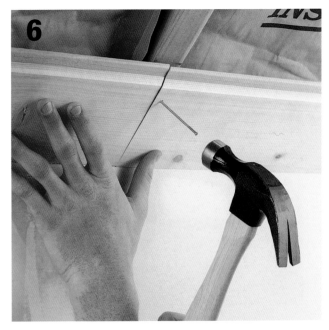

Cut and install any remaining boards in the starter row one at a time, making sure the scarf joints fit together tightly. At each scarf joint, drive two nails through the face of the top board, angling the nail to capture the end of the board behind it. If necessary, predrill the nail holes to prevent splitting.

Cut the first board for the next row, then fit its grooved edge over the tongue of the board in the starter row. Use a hammer and a scrap piece of paneling to drive downward on the tongue edge, seating the grooved edge over the tongue of the starter board. Fasten the second row of boards with blind-nails only.

As you install successive rows, measure down from the peak to make sure the rows remain parallel to the peak. Correct any misalignment by adjusting the tongue-and-groove joint slightly with each row. You can also snap additional control lines to help align the rows.

9

10

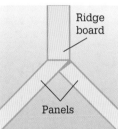

Ridge board

Panels

Rip the boards for the last row to width, beveling the top edges so they fit flush against the ridge board. Face nail the boards in place. Install paneling on the other side of the ceiling, then cut and install the final row of panels to form a closed joint under the ridge board.

Install trim molding along walls, at joints around obstacles, and along inside and outside corners, if desired. (Select-grade 1 × 2 works well as trim along walls.) Where necessary, bevel the back edges of the trim or miter-cut the ends to accommodate the slope of the ceiling.

Tips for Paneling an Attic Ceiling

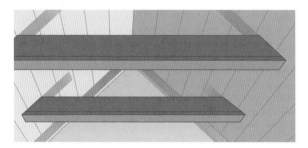

Wrap collar ties or exposed beams with custom-cut panels. Install the paneling on the ceiling first. Then, rip-cut panels to the desired width. You may want to include a tongue-and-groove joint as part of the trim detail. Angle-cut the ends of the trim so it fits tight to the ceiling panels.

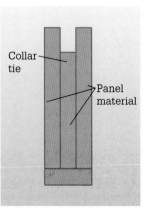

Collar tie

Panel material

Panels

Trim

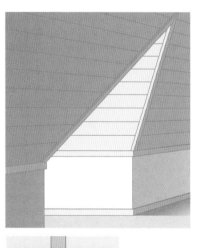

Use mitered trim to cover joints where panels meet at outside corners. Dormers and other attic elements create opposing ceiling angles that can be difficult to panel around. It may be easier to butt the panels together and hide the butt joints with custom-cut trim. The trim also makes a nice transition between angles.

Installing Doors & Windows

In simple terms, installing a standard window or prehung door is merely a matter of positioning the unit in the framed opening, adjusting it so that it's plumb, square, and level, then fastening it to the framing. Making the adjustments can be a little tricky, and there are wall surfaces to consider, but the basic procedure is fairly straightforward—and well within the skill level of most do-it-yourselfers.

You should hang doors after the wallboard or other finish material is in place. The jambs on most prehung doors are the same width as a 2 × 4 framed wall with a layer of ½" wallboard on each side, and having the wallboard in place makes it easier to center the door jambs in the opening so they end up flush with the wall on both sides. Windows also should be installed with the jambs flush with the wall surface, but there are advantages to installing windows early in a project. You may want the added natural light from the windows as you work, or it may be convenient to gain access through a new window.

Skylights essentially are windows in roofs, and framing and installing skylights is similar in many ways to framing and installing standard windows. This section includes a project that shows you how to add a new skylight from start to finish, including building the frame, installing the unit, and adding the all-important flashing, which prevents leaking.

As you read through these projects, keep in mind that there are many types of windows and skylights, as well as exterior wall finishes. Not all of the steps shown in these installation projects will apply to your situation. Therefore, it's important to follow manufacturer's instructions carefully.

After your windows and doors are in place and you've made sure they operate properly, install the interior trim, or *casing*, to complete the project. Most door and window units do not come with casing; it's up to you to select a molding that looks good with the window or door and matches or complements other trim in the room. A good lumberyard or home center will have a variety of casing in several wood species and manufactured materials.

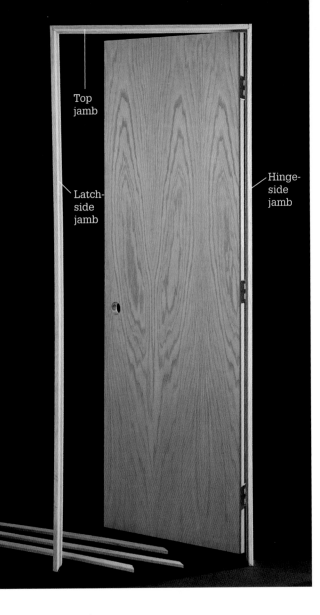

Top jamb

Latch-side jamb

Hinge-side jamb

1" thick jamb extension

If your walls are built with 2 × 6 studs, you'll need to extend the jambs by attaching 1" thick wood strips to the jamb edges on both sides. Use glue and 4d casing nails to attach these extensions to the jambs.

Installing a Prehung Door

Prehung doors come as single units with the door already hung on hinges attached to a factory-built door frame. To secure the unit during shipping, most prehung doors are nailed shut with a couple of duplex nails driven through the jambs and into the door edge. When you're ready to install the door, lean the unit against the wall near the opening, and remove those nails.

The key to installing doors is to plumb and fasten the hinge-side jamb first. After that's in place, you can use the door to position the top and latch-side jambs, by checking the *reveal*— (the gap between the closed door and the jamb.)

Standard prehung doors have $4\frac{1}{2}$"-wide jambs and are sized to fit walls with 2 × 4 construction and $\frac{1}{2}$" wallboard. If you have thicker walls, you can special-order a door to match, or you can add jamb extensions to a standard-size door.

Tools & Materials   4-ft. level ▪ nail set ▪ handsaw
▪ prehung door unit ▪ wood shims ▪ 8d casing nails

How to Install a Prehung Door

Starting near the top hinge, insert pairs of shims driven from opposite directions into the gap between the framing and the jamb, sliding in the shims until they are snug. Check the jamb to make sure it remains plumb and does not bow inward. Install shims near each hinge.

Set the door unit into the framed opening so the jamb edges are flush with the wall surfaces and the unit is centered from side to side. Using a level, adjust the unit so the hinge-side jamb is plumb.

Anchor the hinge-side jamb with 8d casing nails driven through the jamb and shims and into the framing. Drive nails only at the shim locations.

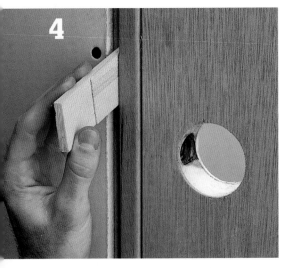

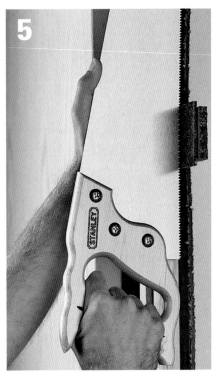

Set all nails below the surface of the wood with a nail set, then cut off the shims flush with the wall surface, using a handsaw or utility knife. Hold the saw vertically to prevent damage to the door jamb or wall.

Insert pairs of shims into the gap between the framing members and the top jamb and latch-side jamb, aligning them roughly with the hinge-side shims. With the door closed, adjust the shims so the reveal is ¹⁄₁₆" to ⅛" wide. Drive casing nails through the jambs and shims and into the framing members.

Installing Windows

If you're installing a window in an attic wall or the framed wall of a walkout basement, you'll probably have to remove the exterior wall sheathing and finish material to clear the window opening. The basic techniques for removing wood siding are shown here. If your house has stucco, brick, or aluminum, vinyl, or other type of siding, consult the siding manufacturer or a remodeling professional for help with removal.

Also note that this installation project involves a wood-frame window and a wood-frame wall. Other window types may require different installation methods, as will installing a window in an exposed-masonry wall.

Tools&Materials Drill ▪ chalk line ▪ circular saw ▪ reciprocating saw ▪ 2-ft. level ▪ chisel ▪ stapler ▪ nail set ▪ utility knife ▪ caulk gun ▪ 10d galvanized casing nails ▪ 8d casing nails ▪ 1 × 4, cedar shims ▪ building paper ▪ drip edge ▪ unfaced fiberglass insulation ▪ silicone caulk.

How to Remove Wood Siding

From inside, drill through the wall at the corners of the framed opening. Push casing nails through the holes to mark their locations. For round-top windows, drill several holes around the curved outline.

Measure the distance between the nails on the outside of the wall to make sure the dimensions are accurate. Mark the cutting lines with a chalk line stretched between the nails. Push the nails back through the wall.

Rest the saw on the 1 x 4, and cut along the chalk line, using the edge of the board as a guide. Stop the cut about 1" from each corner to avoid cutting into the framing. Reposition the board, and make the remaining cuts. Be sure to wear safety goggles while cutting through siding.

Tack a straight 1 x 4 to the wall so its edge is flush against the inside of one of the cutting lines. Drive the nails flush with the surface. Set the blade depth on a circular saw to cut through only the siding, taking into account the thickness of the 1 x 4. Note: Use an old saw blade or a remodeling blade, as you're likely to hit nails as you cut through the siding.

Variation: For round-top windows, make curved cuts, using a reciprocating saw or jigsaw. Move the saw slowly to ensure smooth cuts.

Complete the cuts at the corners with a reciprocating saw or jigsaw, being careful not to cut into the framing.

Remove the cut-out wall section. You may want to remove the siding pieces from the sheathing and save them for future use.

How to Install a Window (in a wood frame)

1

Mullion post

Set the window into the frame from the outside. Slide tapered cedar shims (and small wood blocks, if necessary) under the side jambs and mullion post so that the window is centered in the opening from side to side and top to bottom. Use the level to make sure the window is perfectly plumb and level, adjusting the shims as needed.

2

Brick Molding

Trace the outline of the brick molding onto the wood siding. Remove the window, and cut the siding along the outline just down to the sheathing, using a reciprocating saw held at a low angle. For straight cuts, you can use a circular saw set to the depth of the siding, then finish the cuts at the corners with a chisel.

3

Cut 8"-wide strips of building paper and slide them behind the siding and around the entire window frame, then staple them in place. Cut a length of drip edge to fit over the top of the window, and fit its back flange between the siding and sheathing. Use flexible drip edge for round-top windows and rigid drip edge for straight-top units.

4

Reset the window and push the brick molding tight against the sheathing. Use the level to make sure the window is plumb and level, and adjust the shims, if necessary. Drive a 10d galvanized casing nail through the brick molding and into the frame at each corner.

5

From inside, install flat pairs of shims between the window jambs and the frame, spaced every 12". The shims should be snug but not so tight that they bow the jambs. Use a level to check for bowing, then open and close the window to make sure it operates smoothly.

6

At each shim location, drill a pilot hole and drive an 8d casing nail through the jamb and into the frame. Set the nails with a nail set. Trim the shims flush to the frame using a utility knife or a handsaw, then fill the gaps behind the jambs with loosely packed fiberglass insulation.

7

From outside, drive 10d galvanized casing nails, spaced every 12", through the brick molding and into the frame. Set all nails with a nail set. Apply silicone caulk around the entire perimeter where the brick molding meets the siding. Fill all nail holes with caulk.

Installation Variation: Masonry Clips

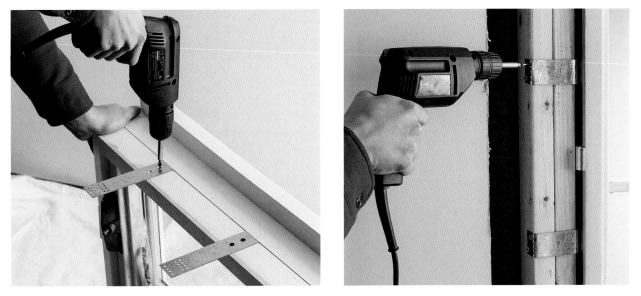

Use metal masonry clips when the brick molding on a window cannot be nailed because it rests against a masonry surface. The masonry clips hook into precut grooves in the window jambs (above, left) and are attached to the jambs with screws. After setting the window in the frame, bend the masonry clips around the framing members and anchor them with screws (above, right). Note: Masonry clips also can be used in ordinary lap siding installations if you want to avoid making nail holes in the surface of the brick molding.

Installing a Skylight

A skylight is a great addition to a finished attic. Depending on the model you choose and where you place it, a skylight can offer warmth in the winter, cooling ventilation in the summer, and a lofty view of the sky or the treetops around your house. And of course, all skylights provide a lot of natural light.

Because a skylight lets in so much light, the sizing and placement of the unit are important considerations. A skylight that's too big (or using too many of them) can quickly overheat a space, especially in an attic. For the same reason, it's often best to position a skylight away from the day's brightest sun. Other ways to avoid overheating include choosing a model with tinted glazing or a low solar-heat-gain coefficient (between .30 and .50), or simply shading the skylight during the hottest hours of the day.

Some attics offer little space for windows and, thus, limited sources of fresh air, so you may want to spend a little more on your skylight and get an operable model that opens and closes. These are good for venting warm air that would otherwise get trapped in the attic, and they help draw cooler air from the floors below.

A skylight frame is similar to a standard window frame. It has a header and sill, like a window frame, but has *king rafters,* rather than king studs. Skylight frames also have *trimmers* that define the sides of the rough opening. Refer to the manufacturer's instructions to determine what size to make the opening for your skylight.

With standard rafter-frame roof construction, you can safely cut into one or two rafters, as long as you permanently support the cut rafters, as shown in this project. If your skylight requires alteration of more than two rafters, or if your roofing is made with unusually heavy material, such as clay tile or slate, consult an architect or engineer before starting the project.

Today's good-quality skylight units are unlikely to leak, but a skylight is only as leakproof as its installation: Follow the manufacturer's instructions, and install the flashing meticulously, as it will last a lot longer than any sealant.

Tools & Materials
4-ft. level ▪ circular saw ▪ drill ▪ combination square ▪ reciprocating saw ▪ pry bar ▪ chalk line ▪ stapler ▪ caulk gun ▪ utility knife ▪ tin snips ▪ 2 × lumber, 16d and 10d common nails ▪ 1 × 4, building paper ▪ roofing cement ▪ skylight flashing ▪ 2", 1¼", and ¾" roofing nails

How to Install a Skylight

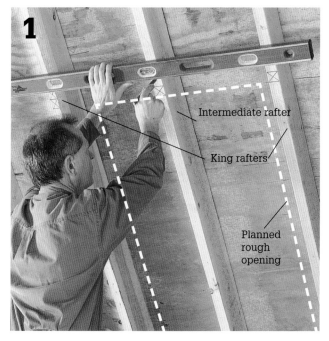

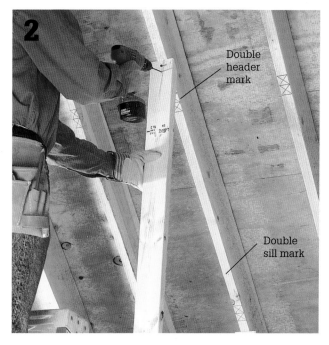

Use the first rafter on each side of the planned rough opening to serve as a king rafter. Measure and mark where the double header and sill will fit against the king rafters. Then, use a level as a straightedge to extend the marks across the intermediate rafter.

Brace the intermediate rafter by installing two 2 × 4s between the rafter and the attic floor. Position the braces just above the header marks and just below the sill marks. Secure them temporarily to the rafter and subfloor with screws.

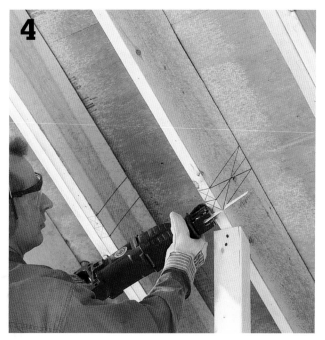

Reinforce each king rafter by attaching a full-length "sister" rafter against its outside face. Cut the sister rafters from the same size of lumber as the existing rafters, matching the lengths and end cuts exactly. Work each sister rafter into position, flush against the outside face of the king rafters, then nail the sisters to the kings with pairs of 10d common nails, spaced 12" apart.

Use a combination square to transfer the sill and header marks across the face of the intermediate rafter, then cut along the outermost lines with a reciprocating saw. Do not cut into the roof sheathing. Carefully remove the cut-out section with a pry bar. The remaining rafter portions will serve as cripple rafters.

Build a double header and double sill to fit snugly between the king rafters, using 2 × lumber that is the same size as the rafters. Nail the header pieces together using pairs of 10d nails, spaced 6" apart.

Cripple rafter

Install the header and sill, anchoring them to the king rafters and cripple rafters with 16d common nails. Make sure the ends of the header and sill are aligned with the appropriate marks on the king rafters.

Trimmers

If your skylight unit is narrower than the opening between the king studs, measure and make marks for the trimmers: They should be centered in the opening and spaced according to the manufacturer's specifications. Cut the trimmers from the same 2 × lumber used for the rest of the frame, and nail them in place with 10d common nails.

When the skylight frame is complete, remove the 2 × 4 rafter braces. Then, mark the opening for the roof cutout by driving a screw through the sheathing at each corner of the frame.

From the roof, measure between the screws to make sure the rough opening dimensions are accurate. Snap chalk lines on the shingles between the screws to mark the rough opening, then remove the screws.

Tack a straight 1 × 4 to the roof aligned with the inside edge of one chalk line. Make sure the nail heads are flush with the surface of the board.

Cut through the shingles and sheathing along the chalk line, using a circular saw and an old blade or a remodeling blade. Rest the saw foot on the 1 × 4, and use the edge of the board as a guide. Reposition the 1 × 4, and cut along the remaining lines. Remove the cut-out roof section.

Remove shingles around the rough opening with a flat pry bar, exposing at least 9" of building paper on all sides of the opening. Remove entire shingles, rather than cutting them.

(Continued next page)

13

Cut strips of building paper and slide them between the shingles and existing building paper. Wrap the paper around so that it covers the faces of the framing members, and staple it in place.

14

Nailing flange

Spread a 5"-wide layer of roofing cement around the roof opening. Set the skylight into the opening so that the nailing flange rests on the roof. Adjust the unit so that it sits squarely in the opening.

15

Nail through the nailing flange and into the sheathing and framing members with 2" galvanized roofing nails spaced every 6". Note: If your skylight uses L-shaped brackets instead of a nailing flange, follow the manufacturer's instructions.

16

Adhesive strip

Patch in shingles up to the bottom edge of the skylight unit. Attach the shingles with 1¼" roofing nails driven just below the adhesive strip. If necessary, cut the shingles with a utility knife so that they fit against the bottom of the skylight.

Skylight jamb

Side flange

Sill flashing

Spread roofing cement on the bottom edge of the sill flashing, then fit the flashing around the bottom of the unit. Attach the flashing by driving ¾" galvanized roofing nails through the vertical side flange (near the top of the flashing) and into the skylight jambs.

18

Step flashing

5" Overlap

Drip edge

Spread roofing cement on the bottom of a piece of step flashing, then slide the flashing under the drip edge on one side of the skylight. The step flashing should overlap the sill flashing by 5". Press the step flashing down to bond it. Do the same on the opposite side of the skylight.

Patch in the next row of shingles on each side of the skylight, following the existing shingle pattern. Drive a 1¼" roofing nail through each shingle and the step flashing and into the sheathing. Drive additional nails just above the notches in the shingles.

Continue applying alternate rows of step flashing and shingles, using roofing cement and roofing nails. Each piece of flashing should overlap the preceding piece by 5".

At the top of the skylight, cut and bend the last piece of step flashing on each side, so the vertical flange wraps around the corner of the skylight. Patch in the next row of shingles.

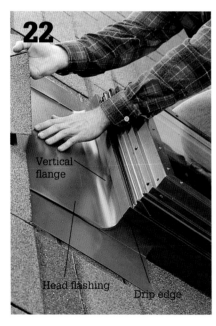

Spread roofing cement on the bottom of the head flashing, to bond it to the roof. Position the flashing against the top of the skylight so the vertical flange fits under the drip edge and the horizontal flange fits under the shingles above the skylight.

Fill in the remaining shingles, cutting them to fit, if necessary. Attach the shingles with roofing nails driven just above the notches.

Apply a continuous bead of roofing cement along the joint between the shingles and skylight. Finish the interior of the framed opening as desired.

Installing Door & Window Casing

Casing is the decorative molding that covers the gaps around the edges of door and window jambs. You can find casing in almost any style and in many different materials, including pine, hardwoods, and manufactured materials. If you'll be painting wood casing, use *finger-jointed* material, which is made from small pieces of pine assembled with finger joints: It's less expensive than standard casing, and you can't tell the difference once it's painted.

In most cases, it's easier to paint the walls before you install the casing. You can also save time by applying primer to casing you'll be painting, or by staining the casing before cutting or installing it. After it's installed, paint the casing or apply touch-up stain to cover any bare wood.

To ensure precise miter cuts that make tight joints, use a power miter saw, if you have one; otherwise, make cuts with a miter box and backsaw.

Tools & Materials Straightedge ▪ power miter saw or miter box and backsaw ▪ drill ▪ nail set ▪ Casing, 6d and 4d finish nails ▪ wood putty

How to Install Casing

On the front edge of each jamb, mark a reveal line to represent the inside edge of the casing. The typical reveal is around ⅛". You can set the reveal anywhere you like, but make sure it's equal on all jambs. Mark light pencil lines just at the corners, or use a straightedge to draw longer lines.

Place a length of casing along one side jamb, flush with the reveal line. At the top and bottom of the molding, mark the points where the horizontal and vertical reveal lines meet (with doors, mark the top ends only).

Make 45° miter cuts at the ends of the moldings. Measure and cut the second vertical molding piece, using the same methods.

Tack each vertical piece in place with two 4d finish nails driven through the casing and into the jamb. Drill pilot holes for the nails to prevent splitting. Do not drive the nails flush at this step.

Measure between the vertical pieces, and cut the top and bottom pieces to length. If the joints don't fit well, move the molding pieces slightly, or make new cuts. When all of the pieces fit well, attach the casing to the jambs with 4d finish nails, spaced every 12" to 16". Then, drive 6d finish nails through the casing near the outer edge and into the wall framing.

Lock-nail the corner joints by drilling a pilot hole and driving a 4d finish nail through each corner, as shown. Drive all nail heads below the wood surface, using a nail set, then fill the nail holes with wood putty.

Installing a Wet Bar

A wet bar typically consists of a small set of cabinets, a countertop, and a sink—a convenient setup for serving drinks or snacks. But by expanding on this basic theme, you can build a bar that brings several amenities of a kitchen right into your new family room or home theater. In addition to providing a place to serve drinks, the new bar will be great for microwaving popcorn or grabbing a cold drink during halftime or movie intermissions.

This project shows you how to build a wet bar that includes a countertop with plenty of room for appliances (and a nearby GFCI receptacle), an under-counter refrigerator/freezer, four full-size cabinets, and a set of elegant glass shelves. At $2 \times 6\frac{1}{2}$ ft., the bar can fit easily into a corner or along a wall. Low-voltage halogen lights placed under the cabinets provide task lighting while additional lights above accent the bar without brightening the room too much.

To begin planning the project, review *Making Preparations*, on page 215. This gives you an overview of the framing requirements and the plumbing and wiring rough-ins needed for the bar. Be aware that the project involves several plumbing connections, as well as some basic wiring. If you aren't familiar with these procedures, consult good books on the subjects, or hire a professional to complete the rough-ins and make the final connections.

After you've made the preparations, follow the step-by-step instructions to install the cabinets, shelves, countertop, and sink, then complete the plumbing and wiring connections, and install the cabinet lights.

Careful placement of the bar will help the project go more smoothly. Wiring can go almost anywhere, but plumbing requires more consideration: To save time and money, locate the bar as close as possible to existing plumbing lines. Also, the fixtures and configurations in this project may not meet code requirements in your area, so have your project plans reviewed by a local building inspector before you start.

Tools & Materials 4-ft. and 2-ft. level ▪ chisel ▪ drill ▪ hole saw ▪ utility knife ▪ nail set ▪ circular saw ▪ compass ▪ belt sander ▪ jig saw and laminate blade ▪ caulk gun ▪ channel-type pliers ▪ framing square ▪ wallboard finishing tools ▪ combination tool (for wiring) ▪ 2 × 4 lumber ▪ 16d common nails ▪ 1½" drain pipe and fittings ▪ ¾ × ½" reducing T-fittings ▪ ½" copper pipe ▪ shutoff valves ▪ escutcheons ▪ electrical boxes ▪ 12/2 and 14/2 NM cable ▪ 20-amp GFCI receptacle ▪ 20-amp receptacle ▪ 15-amp single-pole switch ▪ low-voltage lighting kit ▪ wire connectors ▪ coverplates w/knockouts ▪ cable clamps ▪ ½" wallboard ▪ wallboard finishing materials ▪ primer ▪ paint ▪ cabinets ▪ duct tape ▪ 2½" sheet metal screws ▪ shelf brackets ▪ glass shelves ▪ cedar shims ▪ construction adhesive ▪ toe-kick molding ▪ finish nails ▪ ¾" plywood ▪ wallboard screws ▪ masking tape ▪ silicone caulk ▪ bar sink ▪ faucet ▪ sink-drain assembly ▪ supply tubes

Making Preparations

Note: Always shut off the water supply before working with plumbing. Shut off electrical power at the main service panel and test for power with a circuit tester before doing any electrical work.

The frame requirements for your wet bar depend upon its location. If the back of the bar is set against a masonry wall, the bar will need a framed back wall for holding plumbing and wiring. If the bar is set against an existing framed wall, you may be able to run the service lines through that framing. If the wall is load-bearing, be sure to follow local code requirements for notching and boring into framing.

Before you start the framing, you'll need to plan the rough-ins. If the bar is going in the basement, you may have to break up a portion of the concrete floor to run the drain line for the sink.

You'll also need to know the dimensions of the fixtures going into the wet bar so you can determine the size of the frame. Confirm with the manufacturers the exact dimensions of the cabinets, appliances, fixtures, and countertop you've chosen. Be sure to add the thickness of the wallboard when sizing the frame.

Building the frame itself is simple (see drawing, right). Construct standard 2 × 4 partition walls, with single bottom and top plates, using 16"-on-center spacing. Use pressure-treated lumber for the bottom plates if the bar is in the basement.

It's very important that the framing of the wet bar walls be square: The side walls must be perpendicular to the back wall and parallel to each other. This affects how well the cabinets and countertop fit. Since the side walls of the bar are short, you can use a framing square to check them.

The wet bar in this project has a 12" space above the wall cabinets, which is typical with standard cabinets installed under 8-ft.-high ceilings. You can leave this space open and use it for accent lighting or as a display shelf, or enclose the space with a framed soffit, as is common in most kitchens.

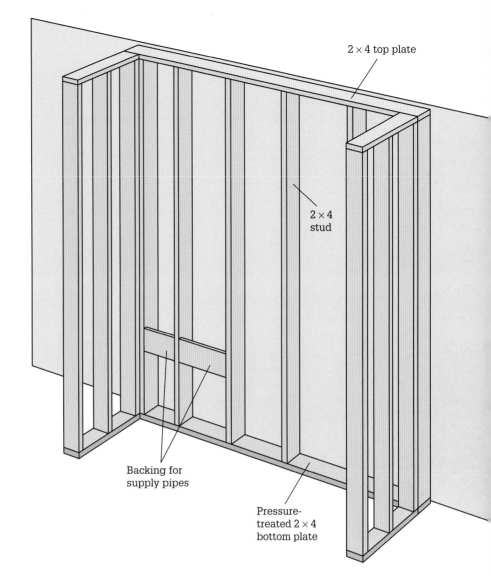

2 × 4 top plate

2 × 4 stud

Backing for supply pipes

Pressure-treated 2 × 4 bottom plate

After the frame is built, complete the plumbing and electrical rough-ins. First, install the drain and vent pipes for the bar sink. Run 1½" drain pipe from the sink location to the main stack or other waste/vent pipe. In a basement, this may require cutting into and breaking up a section of the concrete floor. Set the height of the drain stub-out as required by local code (typically 19" above the floor). Remember that most horizontal drain runs must have a downward slope of ¼" per foot.

According to most codes, sinks must be ventilated within 3½ ft. of the fixture's drain trap. If the waste/vent pipe is within this limit, it can serve as both drain and vent for the sink. Otherwise, you'll need a 1½" vent pipe that extends up and over to the nearest acceptable vent. The new vent pipe must extend upward a minimum of 6" above the flood level of the sink before turning to begin a horizontal run.

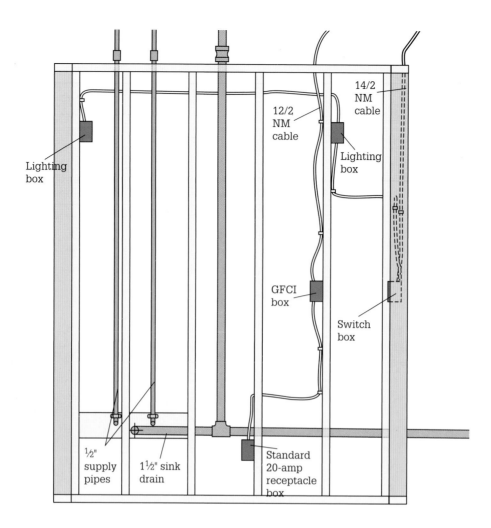

Lighting box

12/2 NM cable

14/2 NM cable

Lighting box

GFCI box

Switch box

½" supply pipes

1½" sink drain

Standard 20-amp receptacle box

To provide hot and cold water to the sink, tap into the nearest water distribution lines with ¾" × ½" reducing T-fittings. Run ½" supply pipes from the fittings to the sink location. Complete the supply stub-outs with an angle stop shutoff valve on each supply pipe. The stub-outs should be spaced about 8" apart.

Install five electrical boxes: one for a single-pole switch, centered 45" above the floor; one for the refrigerator receptacle, centered 12" above the floor; one for the over-counter GFCI receptacle; and one for each cable leading to the low-voltage lighting transformers, located just above the tops of the wall cabinets.

Next, run cable to the boxes. Lighting for the bar is supplied by one 14/2 cable that can be branched from an existing 15-amp lighting circuit. Run the cable to the box for the switch, then run a branch cable from the switch box to the box for the first

transformer. Run another cable between the transformer boxes.

To prevent circuit trippings that would shut off the refrigerator, wire the two receptacles on a dedicated 20-amp circuit. Run 12/2 cable from the service panel to the GFCI receptacle box, then add a branch cable leading to the box for the standard 20-amp receptacle.

Install metal protector plates where pipes and cables pass through framing. After the framing and rough-ins have been inspected and approved, cover the walls and ceiling of the bar with ½" wallboard. Tape and finish the wallboard so the surfaces are completely smooth and flat. Apply primer, then paint the walls and ceiling the color of your choice.

Complete the wiring connections for all devices except the low-voltage lights. Install each device in its electrical box, and attach the coverplate.

Install the Cabinets & Countertops

Draw layout lines for both sets of cabinets. First, use a level to determine if the floor is even. If not, make a mark on the wall near the high point of the floor. Measure straight up from the high point and make a mark for the base cabinets at $34\frac{1}{2}$". Make a mark for the wall cabinets at 84". Use the level to draw level lines through each of these marks to indicate the top edges of all four cabinets (**photo 1**). Also mark the stud locations just above each level line.

Install the coverplates onto the lighting-cable boxes, feeding the cable ends through the clamps in the coverplates and clamping them in place. Prepare the wall cabinets by installing the transformers and fixture wires. Mount one transformer on the top of each wall cabinet with screws. Create a recess for the fixture wires by chiseling a small channel into the back of the support strips at the top and bottom of each wall cabinet. Connect the fixture wires to the transformer, lay them in the channels, and hold them in place with tape (**photo 2**).

Have a helper position one wall cabinet against the back and side walls, aligning its top edge with the upper layout line. Drill pilot holes through the hanging strips inside the cabinet and into the wall studs. Fasten the cabinet to the wall with $2\frac{1}{2}$" sheet metal screws (**photo 3**). Install the remaining wall cabinet against the opposite side wall.

Measure up from the bottom edge on the inside face of each wall cabinet, and make light pencil marks to indicate the height of each shelf bracket. Use a level to make sure the marks are aligned and level. Drill holes for the bracket posts and install the brackets (**photo 4**). Measure between the brackets to determine the length of the glass shelves. Have the shelves cut about $\frac{1}{8}$" short so that you can install them easily.

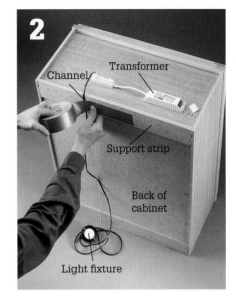

Lay the fixture wire into the channels on the back of each wall cabinet, and secure them with duct tape.

Measure up from the floor's high point, and draw level lines for the tops of both sets of cabinets.

Set each wall cabinet against the back and side walls, and attach it with screws.

Drill holes to accept the posts of the shelf brackets, then push the brackets into place.

(Continued next page)

To set the sink base cabinet, measure the locations of the plumbing stub-outs and transfer the measurements to the back panel of the cabinet. Cut the holes for the stub-outs, using a drill and hole saw (**photo 5**). If necessary, use a jigsaw to cut the hole for the drain stub-out.

Set the sink base cabinet in place. Where necessary, slide tapered cedar shims under the cabinet's bottom edges until the cabinet is aligned with the layout line and is perfectly plumb from front to back (**photo 6**). Apply a small amount of construction adhesive to the shims to hold them in place. Fasten the cabinet to the wall studs, as with the wall cabinets. Install the remaining cabinet against the opposite side wall.

When the adhesive on the shims has dried, cut off the shims flush with the cabinets, using a utility knife. Install the toe-kick molding supplied by the manufacturer. Position the molding flush along the floor, with the ends flush with the cabinet sides. Drill pilot holes through the toe-kicks, and fasten them to cabinets with finish nails (**photo 7**). Set the nails with a nail set.

Install a ¾"-thick × 2"-wide plywood support cleat to the back wall between the base cabinets, keeping the cleat ¾" above the layout line. Then, attach ¾"-thick × 2"-wide plywood buildup strips to the front and back edges of the cabinets. The strips keep the bottom of the countertop's front edge level with the top of the cabinets so they don't hang over the drawer fronts. Fasten the strips flush with the outside edges of the cabinet, using wallboard screws driven through pilot holes (**photo 8**).

Cut holes through the back panel of the sink base cabinet for plumbing lines, using a hole saw.

Shim under the sink base cabinet so that it is perfectly plumb and is aligned with the layout line.

Trim the shims, and install the toe-kick molding with finish nails driven through pilot holes.

Buildup strip   Support cleat

Install a plywood support cleat and buildup strips to provide support for the countertop.

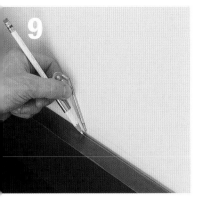

Set the countertop. If necessary, scribe the backsplash with a compass.

Sand the backsplash so it fits tight to the back wall.

Draw the sink cutout onto the countertop, then make the cut with a jigsaw.

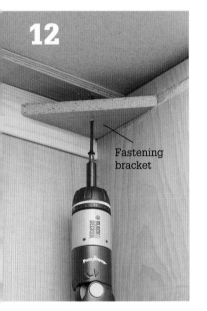

Fastening bracket

Secure the countertop through the cabinet brackets.

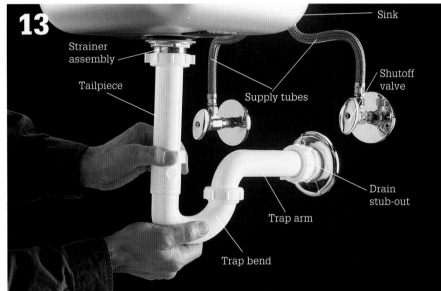

Strainer assembly

Tailpiece

Sink

Supply tubes

Shutoff valve

Drain stub-out

Trap arm

Trap bend

Install the sink in the countertop, connect the water supply tubes to the faucet, and complete the drain assembly.

Set the countertop onto the cabinets. Check to see how the backsplash meets the back wall: If there are any gaps over $\frac{1}{16}$", scribe the backsplash with a compass. Set the compass to the width of the widest gap, then run it along the wall to transfer the wall contours onto the backsplash (**photo 9**). Remove the countertop and sand the edge of the backsplash down to the scribed line. Use a belt sander, holding it parallel to the backsplash to prevent chipping (**photo 10**).

Make the sink cutout, using the sink template. Place strips of masking tape on the countertop, then trace around the template with a pencil. Apply tape to the foot of a jig saw to prevent scratching. Drill a starter hole just inside the cutting line, then com-plete the cutout with the saw. Use a laminate blade or a down-cutting blade, and cut from the finished side of the countertop (**photo 11**). After cutting around each corner, drive an angled screw into the edge of the cutout piece, to keep the piece from falling before the cut is complete, which could chip the laminate.

Reset the countertop, and secure it in place by driving wallboard screws up through the fastening brackets in the cabinet corners (and the buildup strips) and into the particleboard core of the counter-top (**photo 12**). Make sure the screws are not long enough to puncture the laminate surface. Complete the countertop installation by sealing all joints along the wall with a thin bead of silicone caulk.

(Continued next page)

Turn on the lights and experiment with different positions to find the best locations.

Install the Sink & Faucet

Install the faucet, following the manufacturer's instructions. Attach the sink strainer assembly to the sink, then install the sink in the countertop, following the manufacturer's instructions. Be sure to include a watertight seal under the sink rim, using caulk or plumber's putty. Connect flexible supply tubes between the faucet tailpieces and the appropriate shutoff valves. Tighten the connecting nuts with channel-type pliers.

To complete the drain hookup, attach a drain tailpiece to the strainer, then attach a trap arm to the drain stub-out, making the connection with a threaded coupling and a slip washer and nut. Slide the long end of a trap bend (P-trap) onto the tailpiece until

the short end meets the opening of the trap arm. Secure the pieces together with slip washers and nuts. Hand-tighten the nuts (**photo 13**).

Set the Shelves & Lighting Fixtures

Install the glass shelves. Connect the circuit cables to the lighting transformers, following the manufacturer's instructions. With the lights on, position the light fixtures in the desired locations (**photo 14**). Turn off the lights, and attach them to the cabinets with screws. Finally, staple the fixture wires to the bottoms of the cabinets.

Making the Electrical Connections

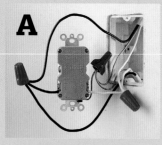

Connect the GFCI receptacle so that it protects itself but not the receptacle for the refrigerator. Pigtail the hot wires to the HOT LINE terminal, and pigtail the neutral wires to the WHITE LINE terminal. Pigtail the grounding wires to the GFCI's grounding screw .

Connect the 20-amp refrigerator receptacle to the wires from the branch cable.

Note: Turn off the power at the main service panel, and use a circuit tester to confirm the power is off before working with electrical cables.

Install the single-pole switch with middle-of-run wiring configuration. Attach one hot wire to each screw terminal, and join the neutral wires together with a wire connector. If the switch has a grounding screw, pigtail the ground wires to the grounding screw. If there's no grounding screw, join the two grounding wires with a wire connector.

Installing a Recessed Kneewall

One great way to utilize the space behind an attic kneewall is to install custom-made storage units. This recessed shelf cabinet provides over nine sq. ft. of storage area without taking up any floor space. And it's a simple project to build using standard materials and basic hand and power tools.

Support for the shelving cabinet is provided by a framed rough opening (similar to a window frame) and two pedestals made from 2 × 4s that sit below the cabinet behind the wall framing. It's best to build the rough opening and pedestals while you frame the kneewall. The main part of the cabinet is made of plywood. A face frame made of solid lumber dresses up the front edges of the cabinet and hides gaps around the wall opening. The drawings on page 222 show you all of the parts needed for the project, and the cutting list includes the materials and dimensions of each part of the project shown.

The type of lumber you use for your shelves depends on how you want to finish them. If you'll be painting the unit, build the cabinet with A/B plywood, which has one side that's free of defects and is sanded smooth. For the face frame, use a quality-grade softwood, such as pine or aspen, without knots and saw marks.

If you want to stain the wood or apply a clear topcoat to retain the natural color, use finish-grade veneer plywood for the cabinet. Veneer plywoods are commonly available in pine, birch, and oak. Specialty lumberyards also offer veneers in maple, cherry, and other species. You can build the face frame from solid lumber that's the same species as the veneer, or choose a different wood that complements the color and grain of the cabinet material.

Tools & Materials Circular saw ▪ 2-ft. level ▪ drill ▪ framing square ▪ bar clamps ▪ nail set ▪ 2 × 4 lumber ▪ ¾" and ¼" plywood ▪ 1 × 4 and 1 × 2 lumber ▪ shims; 3", 2", and 1" wallboard screws ▪ wood glue; 3" and 1½" finish nails ▪ fine-grit sandpaper ▪ finishing materials ▪ wood putty.

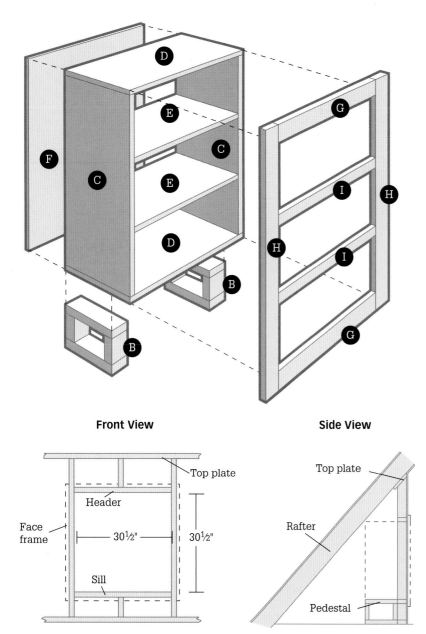

Front View

Top plate

Header

Face frame

30½"

30½"

Sill

Side View

Top plate

Rafter

Pedestal

Frame the Rough Opening & Pedestals

Make the rough opening of the frame ½" wider and taller than the outside dimensions of the cabinet. For the project shown, the rough opening is 30½" wide × 30½" tall. For each side, attach one stud to the top and bottom plates of the kneewall (front view illustration). Attach the sill and header to the side studs, then cut and install cripple studs centered between the side studs. Make sure the studs are plumb and the sill and header are level. You can build your shelving unit to any size, but be sure to leave a few inches of space between the back of the cabinet and the rafters.

Measure from the subfloor to the top of the sill to determine the height of the pedestals (side view illustration). The length of the pedestals should equal the depth of the cabinet minus 4". Build the pedestals with 2 × 4s, then set them on the floor behind the wall so their outside edges are flush with the sides of the rough opening and their tops are flush with the sill. Make sure the pedestals are level, and shim underneath them, if necessary. Attach the pedestals to the subfloor with 3" wallboard screws.

▶ Cutting List

KEY	PART	MATERIAL	PIECES	SIZE
A	Header and sill	2 × 4s	1 each	30½"
B	Pedestals	2 × 4s	2	14 × 15"
C	Sides	¾" plywood	2	19 × 28½"
D	Top and bottom	¾" plywood	2	19 × 30"
E	Shelves	¾" plywood	2	19 × 28½"
F	Back panel	¼" plywood	1	30 × 30"
G	Rails	1 × 4	2	28½"
H	Stiles	1 × 4	2	35½"
I	Shelf rails	1 × 2	2	28½"

Build the Cabinet

If you're building your shelves to match the project shown, cut the top, bottom, and side panels and the shelves using the dimensions shown in the cutting list on page 222 (**photo 1**). If you're custom-sizing your cabinet, measure the width and height of the rough opening, and cut the side panels 2" shorter than the height of the rough opening. Cut the top and bottom panels ½" shorter than the width of the rough opening, and cut the shelves 1½" shorter than the length of the top and bottom panels. Use a framing square to make sure the shelf and panel edges are straight and square.

Measure down from the top of each side panel, and make marks to indicate the top faces of the shelves. You can space the shelves as you like, but make sure the marks are positioned identically on both side panels. Using a framing square, draw lines through the marks on the inside faces of both side panels. Draw lines on the outside faces of the panels, ⅜" below the marks, to indicate the center of the shelves for fastening. Apply wood glue to the short edges of each shelf. Position the shelves against the side panels, aligned with the layout lines, and clamp together the assembly with bar clamps. Drill pilot holes through the side panels and into the shelf edges, and fasten the pieces together with 2" wallboard screws (**photo 2**).

Fasten the top and bottom panels to the short edges of the side panels with glue and screws driven through pilot holes (**photo 3**).

Cut the back panel to size from ¼" plywood. The back panel should match the outer dimensions of the cabinet. Set the back panel over the back of the cabinet so its edges are flush with the outside faces of the bottom, top, and side panels. As you fasten the back panel, adjust the cabinet as necessary so that it's flush with the edges of the back panel. This will ensure that the cabinet is square. Drill pilot holes through the back panel where it meets the edges of the top and bottom panels and the shelves. Attach the back panel with 1" wallboard screws (**photo 4**). Do not use glue to attach the back panel.

Cut the cabinet panels and shelves from ¾" plywood.

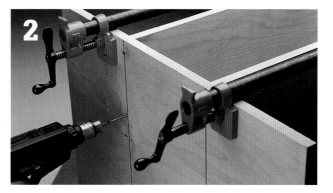

Draw layout lines for the shelves, then attach them between the side panels with glue and screws.

Fasten the top and bottom panels to the ends of the side panels.

Attach the back panel to the back edges of the cabinet, using screws.

(Continued next page)

Assemble the face frame pieces, and reinforce the rail-and-stile joints with toenails.

Attach the face frame to the front edges of the cabinet, using glue and finish nails.

Build & Attach the Face Frame

Cut the stiles and rails to length from 1 × 4 lumber. The stiles should equal the length of the side panels plus 7". The rails and the shelf rails should equal the length of the shelves. Apply glue to the ends of the rails and shelf rails, then assemble the face frame following the drawing on page 222. Position the shelf rails so that their top edges will be flush with the top faces of the shelves. Clamp together the frame, and measure diagonally from corner to corner to make sure the frame is square. If the dimensions are equal, the frame is square. If not, apply pressure to one side of the frame until the measurements are equal. Drill pilot holes, and toenail 3" finish nails through the ends of the rails and into the stiles (**photo 5**). Let the glue dry.

Apply glue to the front edges of the cabinet. Position the face frame over the cabinet so the inside edges of the frame are flush with the side, top, and bottom panels of the cabinet. Drill pilot holes and fasten the frame to the cabinet with 1½" finish nails, driven every 8" (**photo 6**). Set the nails with a nail set.

Finish & Install the Unit

After the glue dries completely, sand the exposed surfaces of the unit with fine-grit sandpaper. Finish the unit as desired.

Set the unit into the wall and center it within the rough opening. Anchor the unit by drilling pilot holes and driving 3" finish nails through the face frame and into the wall studs, header, and sill (**photo 7**). Space the nails evenly, and set the nail heads with a nail set. Fill the nail holes with wood putty and touch up the finish as needed.

Set the unit in place, and secure it with finish nails driven into the wall framing.

Installing a Gas Fireplace

A new gas fireplace with direct venting can be the perfect addition to an attic or basement. Direct venting is a ventilation system that uses a special 2-in-1 vent pipe: The inner pipe carries exhaust fumes outside, while the outer pipe draws in fresh air for combustion. The vent pipe can be routed in many different ways, which means you can install a fireplace in almost any room.

Installing a gas fireplace is a great do-it-yourself project because you can design and build the fireplace frame to suit your needs and add your own finish treatments. It all starts with some careful planning. Once you decide on the fireplace model and determine where to place it, order all of the vent pipes and fittings needed to complete the vent run.

Note: Consult the manufacturer's instructions for the specifications regarding placement, clearances, and venting methods for your fireplace.

Start your planning by determining the best location for the fireplace. Placing the unit next to an exterior wall simplifies the venting required. One important specification for a basement fireplace is that the termination cap (on the outside end of the vent) must be 12" above the ground. In the project shown, the vent runs up 3 ft. before it turns at an elbow and passes through a masonry wall. Because the wall is non-combustible, no heat shield is needed around the vent penetration.

For help with any of these planning issues, talk with knowledgeable dealers in your area. They can help you choose the best fireplace model for your situation and help you with venting and other considerations. And remember, all installation specifications are governed by local building codes: Check with the building department to make sure your plans conform to regulations.

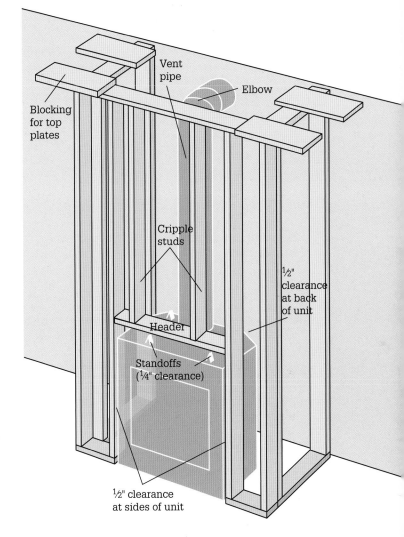

Blocking for top plates

Vent pipe

Elbow

Cripple studs

½" clearance at back of unit

Header

Standoffs (¼" clearance)

½" clearance at sides of unit

Tools & Materials
Framing square ■ chalk line ■ plumb bob ■ circular saw ■ drill ■ 2-ft. level ■ hammer drill ■ masonry bit ■ masonry chisel ■ hand maul ■ adjustable wrenches ■ brush ■ nail set ■ V-notched trowel ■ screwdriver ■ grout float ■ sponge ■ Fireplace unit ■ vent sections ■ termination cap ■ ½" copper tubing, 2 × blocking lumber ■ 2 × 4 lumber ■ construction adhesive ■ masonry fasteners ■ 3" wallboard screws ■ sheet metal plates ■ plastic sheet ■ scrap plywood ■ sheet metal screws ■ caulk ■ ⅝" wallboard ■ wallboard finishing materials ■ high-temperature sealant ■ primer ■ paint ■ mantle ■ wood-finishing materials ■ 6d and 4d finish nails ■ wood putty ■ ceramic tile ■ tile spacers ■ latex tile adhesive ■ masking tape ■ grout ■ cap rail trim ■ buildup strips

Build the Frame

Mark the outer edges of the frame onto the floor. Use a framing square to draw a perpendicular line through each mark to indicate the locations of the side walls. Measure out along these lines and mark the front of the frame, then snap a chalk line through the marks. Measure diagonally from corner to corner to make sure the layout lines are square; adjust the lines, if necessary.

Use a plumb bob to transfer the lines from the floor to the joists above. If any top plates of the frame will fall between parallel joists, install 2 × blocking between the joists. Snap a line through the marks to complete the top-plate layout.

Cut the bottom plates to size from pressure-treated 2 × 4s. Position the plates just inside the layout lines, and fasten them to the floor, using construction adhesive and masonry screws or a powder-actuated nailer. Cut the top plates from standard 2 × 4s, and attach them to the joists or blocking with 3" screws or 16d nails (drill pilot holes for screws) (**photo 1**).

Header

Cut and install the studs, then install the header piece to complete the front opening.

If the plates are attached directly to parallel joists, add backing for attaching the ceiling wallboard.

Mark the stud layout on the bottom plates, then transfer the layout to the top plates, using a plumb bob. Measure to determine the length of each stud, then cut the studs to length. Attach the two studs along the back wall using construction adhesive and masonry screws or a powder-actuated nailer. Attach the remaining studs to the top and bottom plates with 3" screws or 8d nails.

Measure up from the floor and mark the height of the header onto each stud at the side of the front opening. Cut and install the header (**photo 2**). Cut the cripple studs to fit between the header and top plate. To allow easy access for running the vent pipe, do not install the cripple studs until after the vent is in place. Add any blocking needed to provide nailing surfaces for the tile trim.

2 × blocking

Draw layouts for the plates. Attach the bottom plates to the floor and the top plates to the joists.

Position the fireplace inside the frame and, if necessary, install shims to bring it level.

Dry-fit the first section of vent over the vent collars and snap it into place.

Set the Fireplace & Cut the Vent Hole

Bend out the nailing tabs at the sides of the fireplace unit. Slide the unit into the frame until the tabs meet the framing around the opening, then center the unit within the opening. Make sure the unit is level from side to side and front to back, and make any adjustments by shimming underneath with thin sheet metal plates (**photo 3**). Apply a small amount of construction adhesive to the shims to hold them in place. Measure at the sides and back of the unit to be sure the clearance requirements are met.

Dry-fit the vent pieces. Fit the flared end of the first vent section over the vent collars on top of the unit, aligning the inner and outer pipes of the vent with the matching collars (**photo 4**). Push straight down on the vent until it snaps into place over the lugs on the outside of the collar. Pull up on the vent slightly to make sure it's locked into place.

Attach the 90° elbow so that the free end points toward the exterior wall. Note: Horizontal vent runs must slope upward ¼" per foot. If your vent includes additional horizontal sections leading from the elbow, adjust the vent pieces and elbow to follow the required slope. Trace the circumference of the elbow end onto the wall (**photo 5**).

Remove the vent from the unit, and set it aside. Cover the fireplace with plastic and scrap plywood to protect it from debris. Using a long masonry bit and hammer drill, drill a series of holes just outside the marked circle, spacing them as close together as possible. Drill the holes all the way through the block. Be patient; the block cavities may be filled with concrete (**photo 6**).

Mark the position of the vent hole by tracing around the circumference of the elbow.

Drill a series of holes through the block wall, using a hammer drill and long masonry bit.

Carefully knock out the hole, using a masonry chisel and a hand maul. Work inward from both sides of the wall to ensure a clean cutout on the wall surfaces (**photo 7**). Smooth the hole edges, test-fit the horizontal vent piece, and make any necessary adjustments. Uncover the fireplace, and clean up around the unit.

Install the Vent & Test the Fireplace

Reinstall the vertical vent section and elbow, locking the pieces together, as before. To install the adjustable horizontal vent section, measure the distance from the elbow to the termination cap. Adjust the section to length, and secure the sliding pieces together with two sheet metal screws. Install the horizontal vent section and termination cap,

following the manufacturer's instructions. Seal around the perimeter of the cap with an approved caulk (**illustration**).

When the vent run is complete, fasten the fireplace unit to the framing by driving screws through the nailing tabs. Install the cripple studs between the header and top plate.

To make the gas connection, remove the lower grill from the front of the unit. Feed the gas supply pipe into the access hole on the side of the unit, and connect it to the manual shutoff valve (**photo 8**). Tighten the connection with adjustable wrenches.

Turn on the gas supply, and check the connection for leaking by brushing on a solution of soapy water (**photo 9**). Bubbles indicate leaking. If you see bubbles, turn off the gas, tighten the connection, then retest it before proceeding.

Break out the vent hole with a masonry chisel and hand maul, then carefully smooth the rough edges.

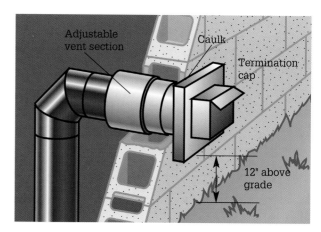

Complete the vent run by installing the adjustable vent section and termination cap. Fasten the cap to the exterior wall and seal around it with caulk.

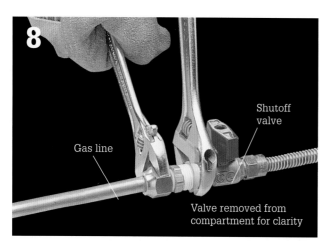

Connect the gas supply line to the manual shutoff valve, and carefully tighten the connection.

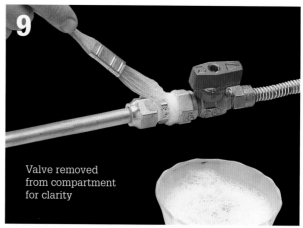

Test the gas connection for leaks by brushing on soapy water and checking for bubbles.

Prepare the firebox, and light the fire, following the manufacturer's instructions. Let the fire run for about 15 to 20 minutes while you inspect the flame and make sure there are no problems with the vent. Report any problems to the manufacturer or dealer. After the test is complete, turn off the fireplace and let it cool down completely.

Apply the Finishes

Install ⅝" wallboard over the framing, running the panels horizontally and attaching them with screws. To provide space for sealant, leave a ⅛" gap between the wallboard and the top and sides of the front face of the unit (**photo 10**).

Fill the gap around the front face with a high-temperature sealant supplied (or recommended) by the manufacturer (**photo 11**). Tape and finish the wallboard seams and inside corner joints, and install

and finish corner bead at the outside corners. Prime and paint the areas of wallboard that won't be covered with tile.

To install the mantle, measure up from the floor and mark the height of the support cleat. Use a level to draw a level line through the mark. Mark the stud locations just above the level line. Position the cleat on the line, centered between the frame sides, and drill a pilot hole at each stud location. Fasten the cleat to the studs with screws provided by the manufacturer (**photo 12**).

Finish the mantle as desired, then fit it over the support cleat, and center it between the frame sides. Holding the mantle tight to the wallboard, drill pilot holes for 6d finish nails through the top of the mantle, about ¾" from the back edge. Secure the mantle to the cleat with four nails (**photo 13**). Set the nails with a nail set, fill the holes with wood putty, then touch-up the finish.

Cover the frame with wallboard, leaving a gap around the black front face of the unit.

Seal around the unit's front face with high-temperature sealant.

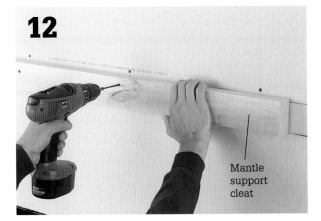

Draw a level line for the mantle support cleat, then attach the cleat to the studs with screws.

Fit the mantle over the cleat, and secure it with finish nails driven through pilot holes.

(Continued next page)

Install the Tile & Trim

Dry-fit the tile around the front of the fireplace. You can lay tile over the black front face, but do not cover the glass or any portion of the grills. If you're using floor tile without spacer lugs on the side edges, use plastic tile spacers to set the grout gaps between tiles (at least ⅛" for floor tile). Mark the perimeter of the tile area and make any other layout marks that will help with the installation (**photo 14**). If possible, pre-cut any tiles.

Using a V-notched trowel, apply latex mastic tile adhesive to the wall, spreading it evenly just inside the perimeter lines. Set the tiles into the adhesive, aligning them with the layout marks, and press firmly to create a good bond (**photo 15**). Install spacers between tiles as you work, and scrape out excess adhesive from the grout joints, using a small screwdriver. Install all of the tile, then let the adhesive dry completely.

Mask off around the tile, then mix a batch of grout, following the manufacturer's instructions. Spread the grout over the tiles using a rubber grout float, forcing the grout into the joints (**photo 16**). Then, drag the float across the joints diagonally, tilting the float at a 45° angle. Make another diagonal pass to remove excess grout. Wait 10-15 minutes, then wipe smeared grout from the tile with a damp sponge, rinsing frequently. Let the grout dry for one hour, then polish the tiles with a dry cloth. Let the grout dry completely.

Cut pieces of cap rail trim to fit around the tile, mitering the ends where the pieces fit together. If the tile is thicker than the trim recesses, install buildup strips behind the trim, using finish nails. Finish the trim to match the mantle. Drill pilot holes and nail the trim in place with 4d finish nails. Set the nails with a nail set (**photo 17**). Fill the holes with wood putty and touch up the finish.

Dry-fit the tile around the fireplace front, and mark the wall to indicate tile positions.

Apply adhesive inside the layout lines, then press the tile firmly into the adhesive.

Force grout into the joints with a grout float, then make two passes to remove excess.

Attach the trim pieces around the tile with finish nails, and set the nails with a nail set.

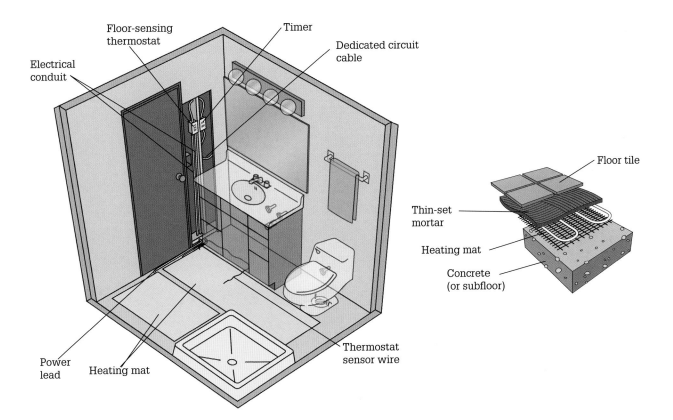

Floor-sensing thermostat

Timer

Dedicated circuit cable

Electrical conduit

Floor tile

Thin-set mortar

Heating mat

Concrete (or subfloor)

Power lead

Heating mat

Thermostat sensor wire

Installing Radiant Floor Heating

Ceramic tile is a great floor covering, but it has a significant drawback: It's cold on bare feet. An easy way to remedy this is to install a floor-warming system.

A typical floor-warming system consists of thin mats containing electric resistance wires that heat up when energized, like an electric blanket. The mats are installed under the floor covering and hard-wired to a 120-volt GFCI circuit. A thermostat controls the floor temperature and a timer turns the system on and off automatically. The systems require very little energy and are designed to heat only the floor. They're not used as a room's sole heat source.

A crucial part of installing this system is to perform several resistance checks to ensure the heating wires have not been damaged. The electrical service required for a floor-warming system is based on its size. If you're installing a new circuit, consider hiring an electrician to make the connection at the service panel.

To order a floor-warming system, contact a manufacturer or dealer. In most cases, you can send in floor plans and the manufacturer will custom-fit a system for your project. The systems can also be used under laminate, vinyl, and floating floors. Don't use them under a wood covering that requires nailing, since the nails can puncture the electric wires. Also, don't use asphalt felt paper as an underlayment. When the paper warms up, it can smell very unpleasant. Use resin paper rather than felt paper.

Tools & Materials
Multi-tester ▪ drill ▪ plumb bob ▪ chisel ▪ tubing cutter ▪ combination tool ▪ vacuum ▪ chalk line ▪ grinder ▪ glue gun ▪ fish tape ▪ aviation snips ▪ ⅜ × ¼" square-notched trowel ▪ tile tools and materials, floor-warming system ▪ 2½ × 4" double-gang electrical box with 4" adapter cover ▪ 2½"-deep single-gang electrical box ▪ ½"-dia. thin-wall conduit ▪ setscrew fittings ▪ 12-gauge NM cable ▪ cable clamps ▪ double-sided tape ▪ electrical tape ▪ insulated cable clamps ▪ wire connectors

Floor-warming systems must be installed on a circuit with adequate amperage and a GFCI breaker (some systems have built-in GFCIs). Smaller systems may tie into an existing circuit, but larger ones often need a dedicated circuit. Follow all local building and electrical codes that apply to your project.

How to Install a Floor Warming System

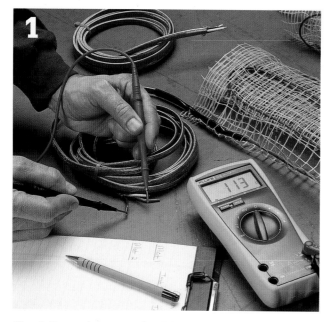

Check the resistance value (ohm) of each heating mat using a digital multi-tester. Record the reading. Compare your reading to the factory-tested reading noted by the manufacturer. Your reading must fall within the acceptable range determined by the manufacturer. If it doesn't, the mat has been damaged and should not be installed. Contact the manufacturer for assistance.

Remove the wall surface to expose the framing. Locate the electrical boxes approximately 60" from the floor, making sure the power leads on the heating mats will reach the electrical box. Mount a 2½"-deep × 4"-wide double-gang electrical box for the thermostat to the wall stud. Mount a single-gang electrical box for the timer on the other side of the stud.

Use a plumb bob or level to mark points on the bottom wall plate directly below the two knockouts on the thermostat box. At each mark, drill a ½" hole through the top of the plate. Drill two more holes as close as possible to the floor through the side of the plate, intersecting the top holes. Clean up the holes with a chisel to ensure smooth routing.

Cut two lengths of ½" thin-wall electrical conduit with a tubing cutter to fit between the thermostat box and the bottom plate. Place the bottom end of each conduit about ¼" into the respective holes in the bottom plate and fasten the top ends to the thermostat box using setscrew fittings. If you're installing three or more mats, use ¾" conduit instead of ½".

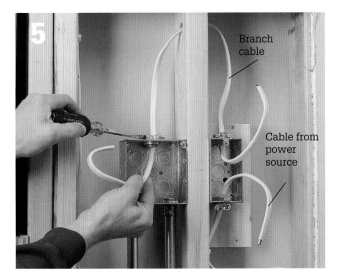

Run 12-gauge NM electrical cable from the service panel (power source) to the timer box. Attach the cable to the box with a cable clamp, leaving 8" of extra cable extending into the box. Drill a ⅝" hole through the center of the stud about 12" above the boxes. Run a short branch cable from the timer box to the thermostat box, securing both ends with clamps. The branch cable should make a smooth curve where it passes through the stud.

Vacuum the floor thoroughly. Plan the ceramic tile layout and snap reference lines for the tile installation (see page 80). Spread the heating mats over the floor so the power leads are close to the electrical boxes. Position the mats 3" to 6" away from walls, showers, bathtubs, and toilet flanges. Place the mats in the kick space of a vanity, but not under the vanity cabinet or over expansion joints in the concrete slab. Set the edges of the mats close together, but don't overlap them. The heating wires in one mat must be at least 2" away from the wires in the neighboring mat.

Confirm that the power leads still reach the thermostat box. Secure the mats to the floor using strips of double-sided tape spaced every 2 ft. Make sure the mats are lying flat with no wrinkles or ripples. Press firmly to secure the mats to the tape.

Create recesses in the floor for the connections between power leads and heating-mat wires, using a grinder or a cold chisel and hammer. These insulated connections are too thick to lay under the tile and must be recessed to within ⅛" of the floor. Clean away any debris and secure the connections in the recesses with a bead of hot glue.

(Continued next page)

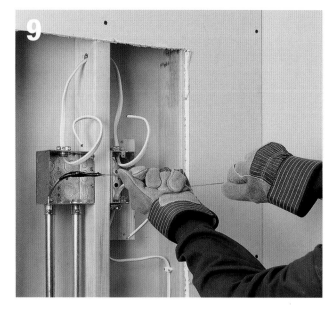

Thread a steel fish tape down one of the conduits and attach the ends of the power leads to the fish tape using electrical tape. Pull the fish tape and leads up through the conduit. Disconnect the fish tape, then secure the leads to the box with insulated cable clamps. Use aviation snips or linesman's pliers to cut off excess from the leads, leaving 8" extending past the clamps.

Feed the heat sensor wire through the remaining conduit and weave it into the mesh of the nearest mat. Use dabs of hot glue to secure the sensor wire directly between two blue resistance wires, extending it 6" to 12" into the mat. Test the resistance of the heating mats with a multi-tester as you did in step 1 to make sure the resistance wires have not been damaged. Record the reading.

Install the floor tile. Using thin-set mortar as an adhesive, spread it carefully over the floor and mats with a ⅜ × ¼" square notched trowel. Check the resistance of the mats periodically as you install the tile. If a mat becomes damaged, clean up any exposed mortar and contact the manufacturer. When the installation is complete, check the resistance of the mats once again and record the reading.

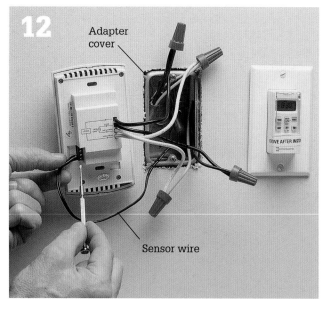

Adapter cover

Sensor wire

Install an adapter cover (mud ring) to the thermostat box, then patch the wall opening with wallboard. Complete the wiring connections for the thermostat and timer following the manufacturer's instructions. Attach the sensor wire to the thermostat setscrew connection. Apply the manufacturer's wiring labels to the thermostat box and service panel. Mount the thermostat and timer. Complete the circuit connection at the service panel or branch connection. After the flooring materials have cured, test the system.

Resources

American Institute of Architects
800-364-9364
www.aiaonline.com

**American Society of
Interior Designers**
202-546-3480
www.asid.org

**Association of Home
Appliance Manufacturers**
202-872-5955
www.aham.org

**National Association of
the Remodeling Industry**
703-575-1100
www.nari.org

National Kitchen & Bath Association (NKBA)
800-843-6522
www.nkba.com

U.S. Environmental Protection Agency Indoor air quality
www.epa.gov/iedweb00/pubs/insidest.html

**International Residential Code (book)
International Conference of
Building Officials**
800-284-4406
www.icbo.com

▶ Metric Conversion Chart

TO CONVERT	TO	MULTIPLY BY
Inches	Millimeters	25.4
Inches	Centimeters	2.54
Feet	Meters	0.305
Yards	Meters	0.914
Square feet	Square meters	0.093
Cubic feet	Cubic meters	0.0283
Quarts (U.S.)	Liters	0.946 (Imp. 1.136)
Gallons (U.S.)	Liters	3.785 (Imp. 4.546)
Pounds	Kilograms	0.454

TO CONVERT	TO	MULTIPLY BY
Millimeters	Inches	0.039
Centimeters	Inches	0.394
Meters	Feet	3.28
Meters	Yards	1.09
Square meters	Square feet	10.8
Cubic meters	Cubic feet	35.3
Liters	Quarts (U.S.)	1.057 (Imp. 0.88)
Liters	Gallons (U.S.)	0.264 (Imp. 0.22)
Kilograms	Pounds	2.2

Photo Credits

Photo Credits (continued)

p. 26-27: Photo Courtesy of VELUX-America.

p. 28: © Brian Vanden Brink for Chris Glass, Architect.

p. 29-30: (both) © Andrea Rugg, photography of walls by Brian Scott Holman.

p. 31: © Andrea Rugg for Newland Architecture.

p. 32: © Brand X Pictures.

p. 33: Photo Courtesy of Velux America.

p. 34: © Arcaid/ Alamy.

p. 35: Photo courtesy of California Closets.

p. 36: © Andrea Rugg for Robert Gerloff Residential Architects.

p. 37: © Elizabeth Whiting and Associates/ Alamy.

p. 38-39: Photo Courtesy of Andersen Windows and Doors.

p. 40: © Andrea Rugg for Tea 2 Architects.

p. 41 (left) : © NordicPhotos/ Alamy.com.

p. 41 (right): Photo courtesy of Dick Blick.

p. 42: © Andrea Rugg for Awad & Koontz Architects Builders, Inc.

p. 43: © Brian Vanden Brink.

pp. 44-45: © Andrea Rugg.

p. 46: (top) © Andrea Rugg for Tea 2 Architects; (bottom) © Brian Vanden Brink for John Libby, Barnmasters.

p. 47: © Andrea Rugg for Tea 2 Architects.

p. 48: Robert Harding Picture Library Ltd, Photolibrary.com

p. 49: (bottom) Photo courtesy of Binkey's Woodworking.

p. 50-51: © Andrea Rugg for Tea 2 Architects.

P: 52: Photo courtesy of Kraftmaid Cabinetry, Inc.

p. 53: © Andrea Rugg for Tea 2 Architects.

p. 54: © Andrea Rugg for Locus Architecture, Cabinets by Thompson Woodworking and Mfg. Co.

p. 55: © David Livingston/ www.davidduncanlivingston.

p. 56: (both) © Andrea Rugg for Locus Architecture.

p. 57: (top) Photo courtesy of The Company Store; (bottom) Photo courtesy of VELUX-America.

p. 58: (top) © Brian Vanden Brink for John Morris Architects; (bottom) © Andrea Rugg.

p. 59: Photo courtesy of VELUX-America.

p. 60: Workbook, Inc./ Photolibrary.com

p. 61: Photo courtesy of Finnleo Sauna and Steam.

p. 62: © Andrea Rugg for David Hiede Design.

p. 63: © Andrea Rugg for Otogawa-Anschel Design and Build.

p. 64: © Brian Vanden Brink.

p. 65-67: (all) © Andrea Rugg for Otogawa-Anschel Design and Build.

p. 68-69: © Brian Vanden Brink.

p. 70: (both) © Andrea Rugg for Locus Architecture.

p. 71: (top) Photo courtesy of IKEA.

p. 72: (top) Photo courtesy of IKEA; (bottom) © Andrea Rugg for Otogawa-Anschel Design and Build.

p. 73: (both) © Andrea Rugg for Otogawa-Anschel Design and Build.

p. 74-75: © Elizabeth Whiting/ Alamy.

p. 76: (top) © Brian Vanden Brink; (bottom) Photo courtesy of IKEA.

p. 77: © Jessie Walker.

p. 78-79: (both) © Andrea Rugg for Quigley Architects.

p. 80: © Andrea Rugg for David Hiede Design.

p. 81: (both) © Andrea Rugg for William Beson Interior Design.

p. 82: © Andrea Rugg for David Hiede Design.

p. 83: © Photo courtesy of Kitchoo.

p. 84: (both) © Andrea Rugg for David Hiede Design.

p. 85: © VIEW Pictures, Ltd./ Alamy.

p. 124: (both) © Bob Perron.

p. 130: (top right) Photo courtesy of The Bilco Company.

p. 133: Photo courtesy of The Bilco Company.

p. 163: © Jeff Krueger.

p. 170: (bottom) Photo courtesy of Heatway Floor & Snow Melting.

p. 174: Photo courtesy of Armstrong Ceilings.

p. 179: (bottom) Photos courtesy of Airvent, Inc.

p. 194: Photo courtesy of Western Red Cedar Lumber Association.

p. 206: Photo courtesy of VELUX-America.

p. 212: (top) Photo courtesy of Andersen Windows.

Index

New from

CREATIVE PUBLISHING INTERNATIONAL

Complete Guide to Basic Woodworking
Complete Guide to Bathrooms
Complete Guide Build Your Kids A Treehouse
Complete Guide to Ceramic & Stone Tile
Complete Guide to Creative Landscapes
Complete Guide to Decks
Complete Guide to Easy Woodworking Projects
Complete Guide to Finishing Walls & Ceilings
Complete Guide to Flooring
Complete Guide to Gazebos & Arbors
Complete Guide to Home Carpentry
Complete Guide to Home Plumbing
Complete Guide to Home Wiring
Complete Guide to Kitchens
Complete Guide to Landscape Construction
Complete Guide Maintain Your Pool & Spa
Complete Guide to Masonry & Stonework
Complete Guide to Outdoor Wood Projects
Complete Guide to Painting & Decorating
Complete Guide to Patios
Complete Guide to Roofing & Siding
Complete Guide to Trim & Finish Carpentry
Complete Guide to Windows & Doors
Complete Guide to Wood Storage Projects
Complete Guide to Yard & Garden Features
Complete Outdoor Builder
Complete Photo Guide to Home Repair
Complete Photo Guide to Home Improvement

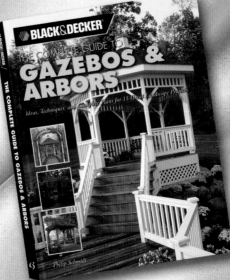

ISBN 1-58923-285-2

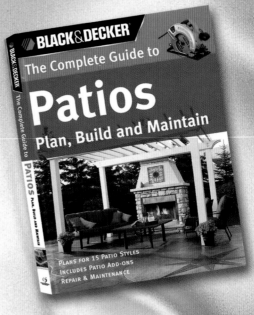

ISBN 1-58923-305-0

CREATIVE PUBLISHING INTERNATIONAL
18705 LAKE DRIVE EAST
CHANHASSEN, MN 55317
WWW.CREATIVEPUB.COM